mentor Lernhilfe

Englisch

5./6. Klasse

Grammatik und Wortschatz:
Grundlagen, Teil 2

Rainer Iwen

Mit ausführlichem Lösungsteil zum Heraustrennen

Special: Lerntipps!

In Zusammenarbeit mit Langenscheidt

mentor
Eine Klasse besser.

Über den Autor:
Rainer Iwen, Realschulrektor und Studienleiter für Englisch am Institut für Praxis und Theorie der Schule (Landesinstitut für Lehrerfortbildung)

Lerntipps:
Alexander Geist, staatlicher Schulpsychologe an einem Gymnasium

Redaktion: Eva-Maria Gärtner

Illustrationen: Jutta Bauer, Hamburg; Christiane Hansen, Hamburg

Layout: Barbara Slowik, München

Umschlaggestaltung: büro schels für gestaltung, München

Umwelthinweis: Gedruckt auf chlorfrei gebleichtem Papier.

Auflage:	8.	7.	6.	5.	4.	Letzte Zahlen
Jahr:	2007	2006	2005	2004	2003	maßgeblich

Satz / Repro: OK Satz GmbH, München
Druck: Landesverlag Druckservice, Linz
Printed in Austria · ISBN 3-580-63541-7

Inhalt

Preface

Vorwort

Dear friend,

wir hoffen, dass du bei der Arbeit mit dem ersten Teil von „Grammatik und Wortschatz" viel Spaß und vor allem Erfolg gehabt hast. Auch der zweite Teil will dir helfen, deine Lücken im Fach Englisch aufzufüllen. Du hast zwei Möglichkeiten, mit dem Buch zu arbeiten:

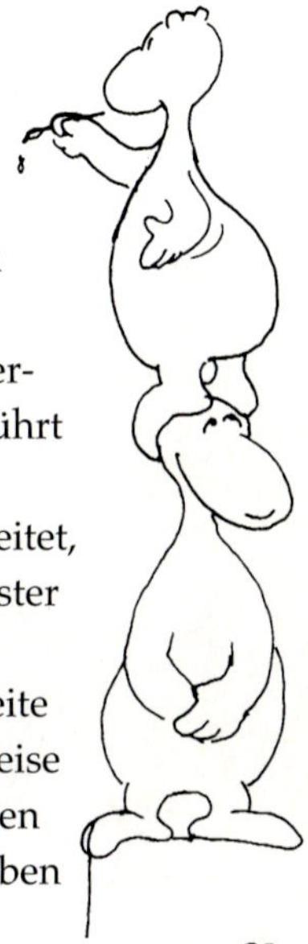

1. Du arbeitest es von vorn bis hinten durch, als Wiederholungskurs zusätzlich zum Unterricht. Das Buch führt dich vom Einfachen zum Schwierigen.
2. Du suchst dir den Stoff, der dir Schwierigkeiten bereitet, aus dem Inhaltsverzeichnis oder dem Stichwortregister heraus und erarbeitest diesen Teil.

Beginne aber jedes Kapitel immer am Anfang und arbeite es bis zum Ende durch. Auch die Kapitel sind stufenweise aufgebaut, sodass du durch die Arbeit mit den Aufgaben Hilfen für die Lösung der weiteren Aufgaben erhältst.

Lies die Einführung zu den Übungen genau durch, denn nur wer eine Aufgabe genau verstanden hat, kann sie auch mit Erfolg lösen.

Schreib auf die vorgegebenen Linien oder – bei längeren Übungstexten – in dein Heft.

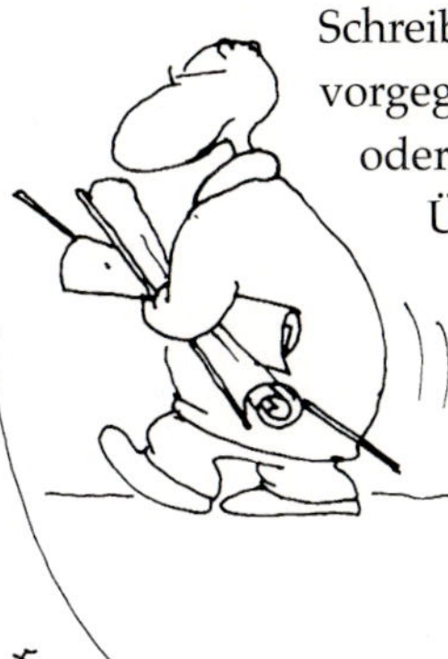

Schreibe in das Buch zunächst mit Bleistift, sodass du später leicht korrigieren kannst. Vergleiche deine Lösung mit dem Lösungsteil und korrigiere deine Fehler. Bearbeite die nächste Aufgabe ebenso. Übersetze nie ins Deutsche – es sei denn, du wirst dazu aufgefordert.
Du wirst dein Wissen festigen, wenn du am Schluss eines Kapitels die Dialoge, Texte und Grammatikregeln auswendig lernst und laut vor dich hin – oder auf eine Kassette – sprichst.
Wir hoffen, dass dir die Arbeit mit dieser „mentor Lernhilfe" Freude macht und dir Erfolg bringt.

Rainer Iwen (Verfasser)

Jutta Bauer (Grafikerin)
Christiane Hansen (Grafikerin)

Übrigens:

Das hier ist Fred. Er wird dir in diesem Buch noch oft begegnen. Fred und eine ganze Reihe von Kindern helfen dir beim Englischlernen.

Benutzerhinweise

Folgende Symbole haben wir im Buch verwendet:

Information: Hier erfährst du Wichtiges über Grammatik oder Wortschatz.

Dialogue: Wenn diese beiden auftauchen, geht es ums Sprechen: Wie kannst du bestimmte Dinge auf Englisch sagen?

Writing: Fred erinnert dich daran, dass du einen Stift brauchst – es geht ums Schreiben, meist von längeren Übungstexten.

Reading: Das Buch zeigt dir, dass es um das Lesen und Verstehen von Texten geht.

Attention: Hier heißt es aufpassen! Hinweise auf Verwechslungsgefahr oder besonders schwierige Satzkonstruktionen.

Unbekannte Wörter findest du sicher hier und da – und manchmal auch Übersetzungen am Rand, in der Bedeutung, die das Wort in diesem Text hat! Wenn du noch mehr Wörter nicht weißt, sie aber unbedingt brauchst, schau in ein Wörterbuch, z. B. das Power Dictionary von Langenscheidt.

Die Rechtschreibung in diesem Band entspricht den Regelungen der Reform.

1. Talking about yourself

Übungsziel: Auskunft über sich selber geben

You already know much about the English language. You'll learn more with this book. Try the following exercise.

Talk about each topic in at least three sentences.

Übungsziel: Gebäude und Einrichtungen einer Stadt benennen können

2. In Town

Ü 2.1. Illustrated vocabulary

Match the words to the buildings and objects in a town. Write the words under the pictures.

park – traffic lights – railway station – bus stop – fountain – cinema – factory – square – office – car park – monument – letterbox – skyscraper – phone box – post office – library – subway – hospital – bench – street-lamp – stadium – avenue – Underground (Tube) – corner – litterbin – tower – police station

Ü 2.2. Where are you going?

Look at the pictures and write suitable answers in the six balloons. Choose from the list below.

suitable – passend

to the post office – to school – to the castle – to the stadium – to the library – to the railway station

Ü 2.3. Buildings in a town

Look at the picture and match the numbers of the buildings to the nouns below.

town:

- 13 newsstand
- bank
- hotel
- cinema
- factory
- park
- school
- church
- car park
- supermarket
- police station
- phone box
- post office
- museum
- public toilets
- station

Ü 2.4. The town of colours

blue	red	green	grey	white
yellow	orange	brown	pink	black

Colour in the town and describe the picture. Write in your exercise book.

My school is pink and yellow. The cinema is red and …

Ü 2.5. Places in town

Search for the words and write them in the blanks.

blank – Lücke, Leerstelle

1. It is a building, where you can see a lot of interesting old things.

   It is a museum.

2. You can read and borrow books there. It is the ______________.
3. It is a big building for sick people. It is the ______________.
4. You can stay there when you are on a journey. It is a ______________.
5. You can watch football matches there. It is a ______________.
6. It is a building where you can buy stamps. It is the ______________.
7. Young people like to go there and study. It is a ______________.
8. Many people work there and produce things. It is a ______________.
9. There are many trains and passengers going on journeys.

   It is the ______________.

10. Burglars and robbers don't like this building. It is the ______________.

Ü 2.6. Over to you

Write sentences in your exercise book.

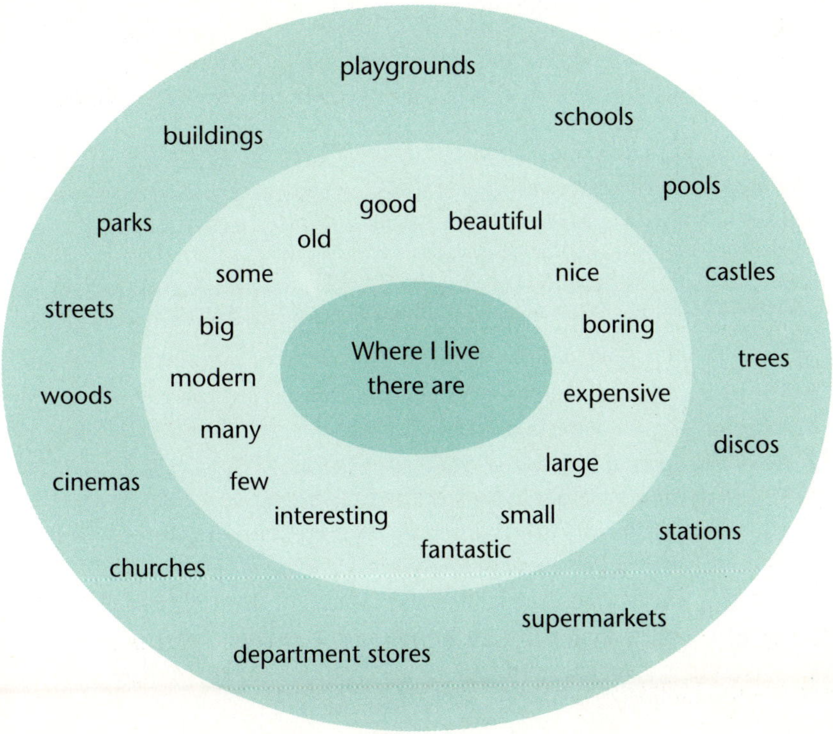

playground – Spielplatz

woods – Wälder

department store – Kaufhaus, Warenhaus

Übungsziel: Fahrzeuge und Transportmittel benennen können

3. Traffic

Ü 3.1. Vehicles

   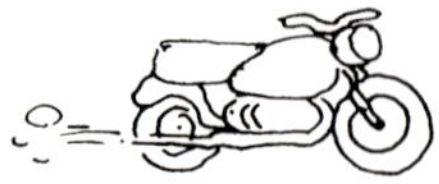

   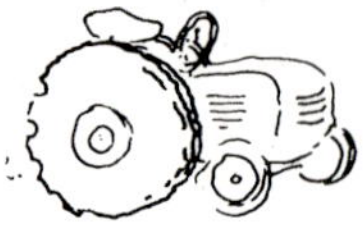

lorry

Put the scrambled letters in the right order and match the descriptions to the pictures. Write under the pictures.

goods – Waren

wheel – Rad
engine – Motor

means of transport – Transportmittel

1. A yorlr is used to transport goods.
2. A sub transports lots of people around the city and the country.
3. A rac is a vehicle with four wheels and an engine.
4. The cilecyb is the favourite means of transport for many young people.
5. The xita is the most expensive means of transport in the city.
6. A feri-gineen is a vehicle used by firemen.
7. An enaralope has got wings and flies in the air.
8. The mrat drives on rails in the city. It stops often.
9. The ircteycl is mostly used by young children. It has got three wheels.
10. A romtokebi is a vehicle with two wheels and an engine.
11. A naitr is a very long vehicle. It drives on rails. It stops at railway stations.
12. A nav is smaller than a lorry. It brings food and drink.
13. A naravac is a vehicle with four wheels without an engine. You can sleep in it on holidays.

14. A catrtro is a vehicle used by farmers. It's very slow and has got two big wheels and two smaller wheels.
15. A ehlicreopt can fly in the air, but it hasn't got wings.

Ü 3.2. Traffic jam

traffic jam – Stau

Count the vehicles and write down how many there are.

There are ________ bicycles. There are ________ lorries.

There are ____.

There are ____.

If you want you may colour in the picture.

Übungsziel: das Verb to go gebrauchen

The verb *to go*

To go ist ein Verb, das für verschiedene Arten der Bewegung benutzt wird. Es bedeutet

1. fahren allgemein: *The train goes fast.*
2. die Fortbewegung von Personen mit Fahrzeugen: *We go to school by car.*

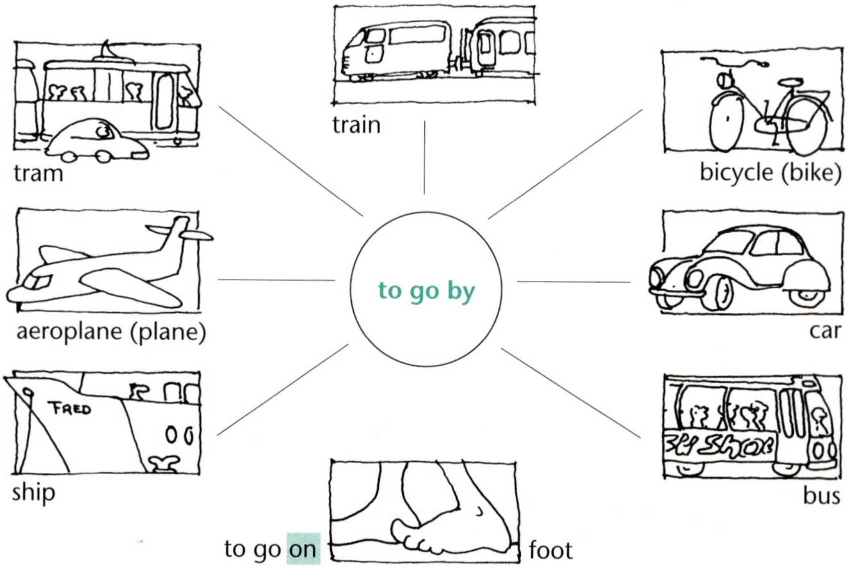

Ü 3.3. Where are they going?

Peter	Brenda	Ricky	Susan	David

London	school	his girl friend	the beach	the post office

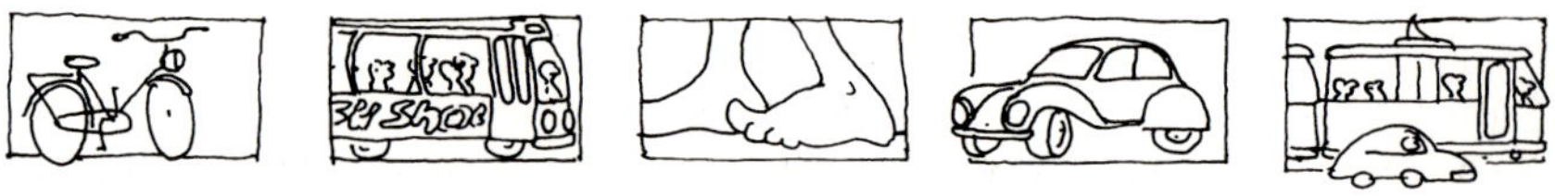

Peter is going to London by bike.

Brenda ______________________.

Ricky ______________________.

Susan ______________________.

David ______________________.

Ü 3.4. A road accident

Read this story about a road accident and look at the pictures. Decide in which order the pictures should be and write down the numbers.

Ricky lives in London. One morning he was on his way to school. Suddenly he had an accident in Oxford Street. He was overtaking a bus that had stopped at a bus stop, then everything happened very quickly. Ricky turned round to look at a Rolls Royce that was behind him. He didn't see an old lady that was crossing the road and knocked her down. Luckily the old lady was not badly hurt. Ricky at once ran to the nearest phone box and called an ambulance. The old lady was taken to the hospital. Later Ricky bought a beautiful bunch of flowers and went to visit her.

accident – Unfall
overtake – überholen

bunch of flowers – Blumenstrauß

This is the right order of the pictures: ☐ ☐ ☐ ☐ ☐ ☐ ☐ ☐

Answer the following questions:

1. Whose fault was it?

____.

2. Why did the accident happen?

____.

to be hurt – verletzt sein

9…9…9 There's been an accident! An ambulance … quick, an ambulance … somebody's hurt!	1	2	3	Where are you phoning from? Tell me your name …
	4	5	6	
	7	8	9	
	#	0	⌦	

ambulance – Krankenwagen

Every day there are about 1500 road accidents in London like this one. Many people are hurt. London's Ambulance Service is there to help these people. An ambulance is not just a large van with a blue light on the top. It's almost like a small hospital.

Ü 3.5. You are a witness

You are on holiday in London and you saw the accident. Some time later the police arrives and asks you a lot of questions.

right of way – Vorfahrt

Questions	**Answers**
Did you see the accident?	Yes, I …
Where did the accident happen?	It happened …
When exactly did it happen?	It happened at …
Was anyone hurt?	Yes, the old …
Who called the ambulance?	The boy …
When did the ambulance arrive?	The ambulance arrived …
Whose fault was the accident?	I think … The lady had the right of way …
Are you from Germany?	Yes, …
What's your name?	My name is …
Where in Germany do you live?	I'm from …
Are you on holiday here?	Yes, …

Read the questions aloud and answer them.
If you have a partner try this exercise with him or her.

Write down the dialogue in your exercise book.

Policeman: Did you see the accident? You: Yes, I was there, when it happened.

4. The Imperative

Übungsziel:
Bejahte und verneinte Befehlsform gebrauchen können

Mit der Befehlsform kann man eine Aufforderung, einen Befehl, eine Bitte, aber auch ein Verbot ausdrücken.
Im Englischen hat der Imperativ immer dieselbe Form wie der Infinitiv des Verbs. Im Befehlssatz steht diese Form am Satzanfang und das Subjekt fehlt.

Positive imperative

subject	predicate	object
Mother	gives	Peter a glass of milk.
	Give	Peter a glass of milk.

Ü 4.1. Instruction game

Follow these instructions.

1. First **read** all the instructions.
2. Draw a line across the box between A and B.
3. Draw a circle above the line.
4. Draw a triangle below the line.
5. Draw a face inside the circle.
6. Write your name under the triangle.
7. Draw a line from A to C.
8. Draw a flower beside the triangle.
9. Stand on your head.
10. Follow instructions two, four and seven **only**.

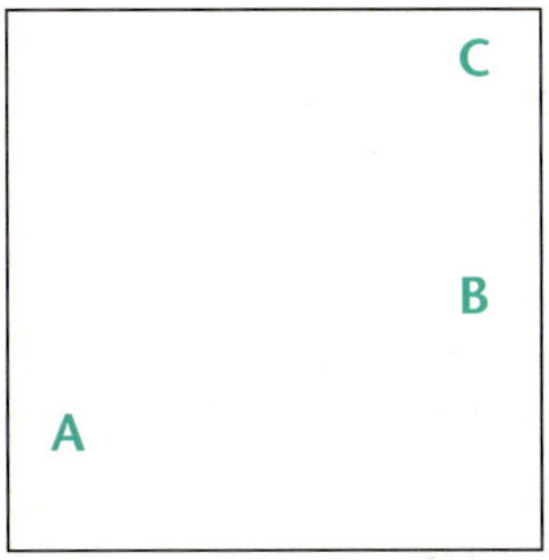

triangle – Dreieck

Ü 4.2. Orders at school

Draw lines between the sentences your teacher says and your reaction.
Write the right letters in the list below.

1 Stop that noise.
2 Open your books.
3 Be quiet.
4 Look at the board.
5 Listen to me.
6 Get out your homework.
7 Keep your books shut.
8 Speak up.
9 Stop playing around.
10 Write down the words.

A Du hörst auf zu spielen.
B Du schaust auf die Tafel.
C Du schließt dein Buch.
D Du schreibst die Wörter auf.
E Du sprichst lauter.
F Du hörst auf zu lärmen.
G Du hörst auf zu schwatzen.
H Du hörst jetzt zu.
I Du holst die Hausaufgaben raus.
J Du öffnest dein Buch.

1	2	3	4	5	6	7	8	9	10

Ü 4.3. Keep fit with Fred

describe – beschreiben
order – Befehl, Anweisung

Look at the pictures, do the described actions and give yourself orders.

stand up

sit down

lift your left foot

touch your nose

jump up and down

lift your left arm

touch your head

lie down

Tell your friend what to do. Use the imperative of the following verbs:

put – jump – touch – lie – bend – lift – stand – sit

bend – beugen

Negative imperative

Den verneinten Imperativ bildet man, indem man die Kurzform *don't* vor den Infinitiv des Verbs stellt.

don't	+	Infinitiv

Don't go out.
Don't play with that dog.

Ü 4.4. A boy good for nothing

boy good for nothing – Tunichtgut

Tom is a boy good for nothing. What is his mother shouting?

Write sentences:

cut

Don't cut up the magazine.

open

______________________________.

throw out

______________________________.

climb

______________________________.

write

______________________________.

cross

______________________________.

Ü 4.5. An angry teacher

Mr. Teabody is very angry. What does he tell the children?
Write sentences in your exercise book. Use the verbs below.

window pane – Scheibe

play – draw – write – do – look – stand

Mr. Teabody says: Don't throw paper planes! Don't …

Ü 4.6. Signs in town

sign – hier: Schild

Where can you see these signs?
Draw lines between the signs and the place.

petrol station – Tankstelle

DO NOT WALK ON THE GRASS	DO NOT BRING ANIMALS WITH YOU	QUEUE THIS SIDE
FASTEN SEAT BELTS	at a petrol station in a zoo on a plane in a park in a train on a door at a bus stop in a library in a shop in a restaurant	PUSH PULL
DON'T FEED THE ANIMALS		BRING YOUR FRIENDS
BE QUIET PLEASE	DO NOT LEAN OUT OF THE WINDOW	DON'T SMOKE

Requests

Wenn man eine oder mehrere Personen auffordert, mit einem selbst zusammen etwas zu tun, dann beginnt diese Aufforderung mit *Let's*.

Let's (= Let us)	+	Infinitiv

Let's look at the next exercise.

Ü 4.7. Let's do

Look at the pictures and write down sentences.

1. Let's play tennis.

2. ______________________

3. ______________________

4. ______________________

5. ______________________

6. ______________________

art gallery – Gemäldesammlung

7. ______________________

8. ______________________

*Übungsziel:
Nach dem Weg fragen und darauf antworten können*

5. Asking and telling the Way

When asking the way, this is what you ask.

Can you tell me the way to …?
Could you please tell me how to get to …?
Can you tell me where … is?
How do I get to …?
Which is the shortest / quickest way to …?
Is there a bus to …?
How far is it to …?

When telling the way your description must be clear and understandable. Use the following to help you.

bridge

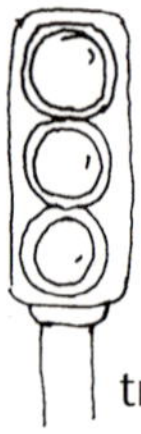

traffic lights

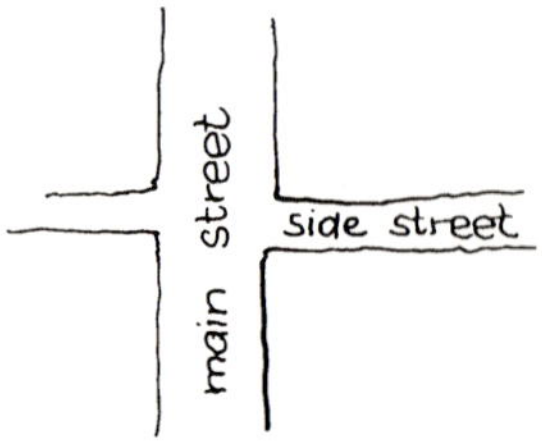

zebra crossing

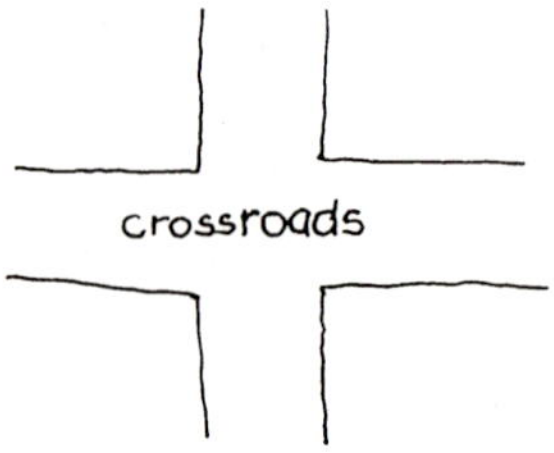

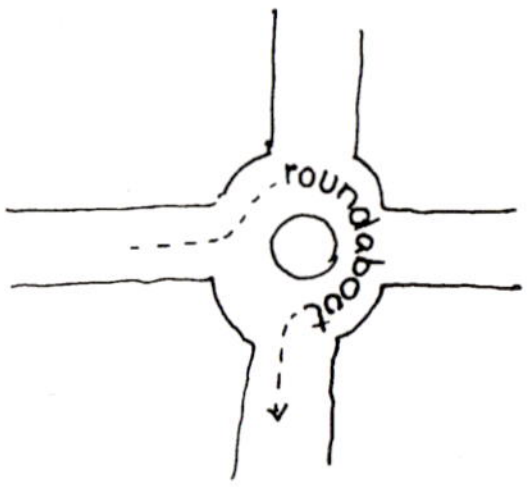

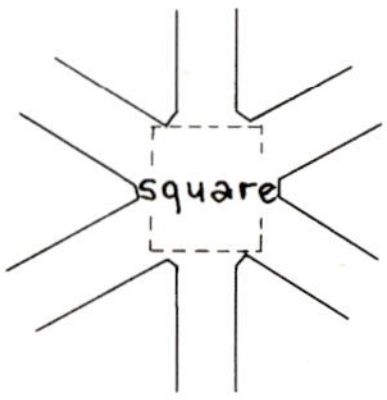

Tell about places, roads signs and buildings in a town.

Count the streets and other things.	the second street the first crossing the third traffic light

Tell how far it is.	It's about … metres, miles, kilometres from … It's a long way to … It's not far from …

Give directions.

Turn left / right — at … / before … / after …

Stop at …

Drive / Walk / Go — past … / along … / through … / as far as … / till you come …

till – bis

Go straight on …

Ü 5.1. Matching exercise

Match the descriptions to the pictures and fill in the right letters below.

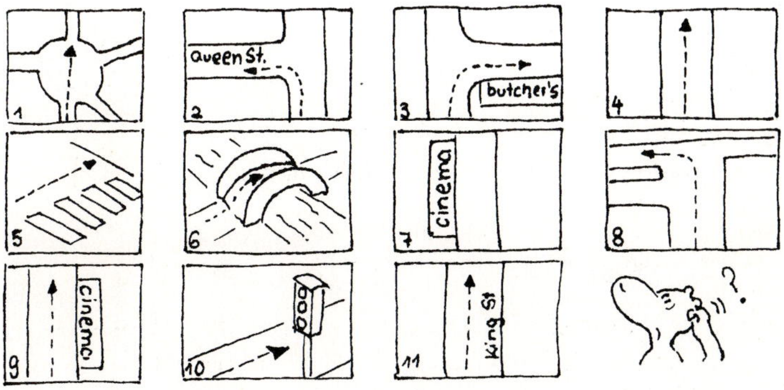

A The cinema is on the left.

B Go across the square.

C Go past the cinema.

D Go as far as the traffic lights.

E Go straight on.

F Turn left into Queen Street.

G Go across the bridge.

H Go across the zebra crossing.

I Go along King Street.

J Turn right at the butcher's.

K Take the second road on the left.

1	2	3	4	5	6	7	8	9	10	11

Ü 5.2. Fred in New York

Can you find Fred in New York? Where is he?
Follow the directions and draw the way on the map. Make a cross where he is.

1. Go across the bridge.
2. Turn into East 125th Street.
3. Go past the post office and cinemas.
4. Go straight on till you come to the traffic lights.
5. Turn round the corner to the left.
6. Go straight on and round the roundabout.
7. Turn right into Green Street.
8. Cross West 127th Street.
9. Go through the gate into Central Park.
10. You'll meet Fred at the first pond.

pond – Teich

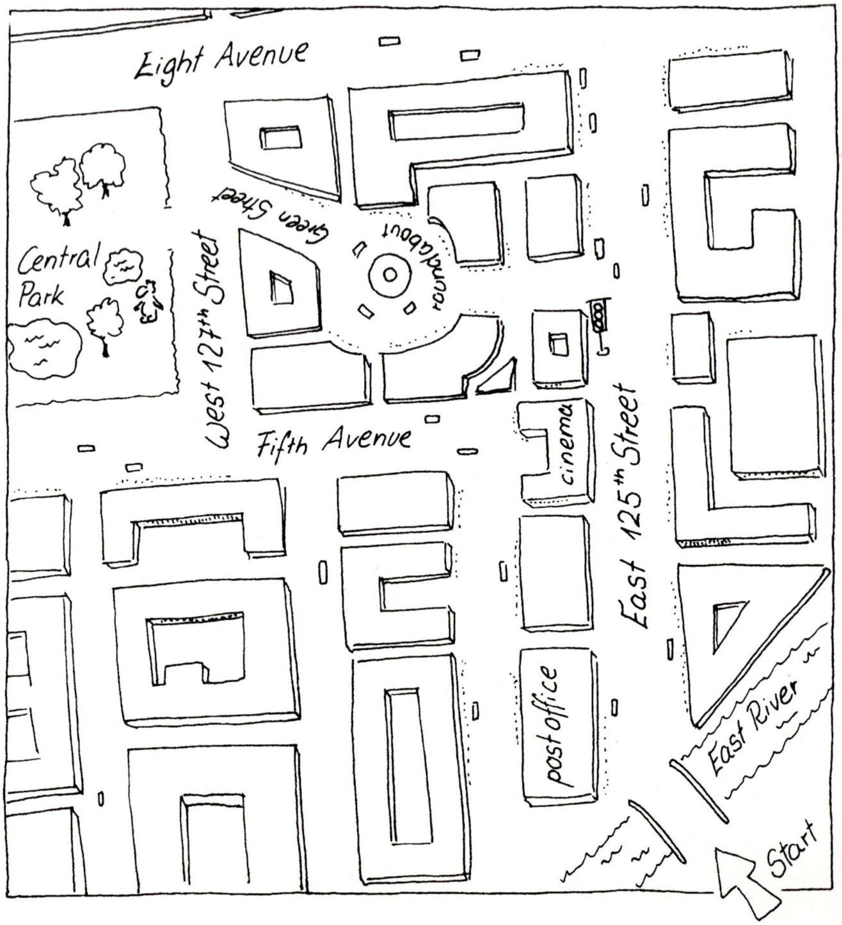

Ü 5.3. Telling the way

Describe the way from the church to the bank.

1. Go ________________ past the ________________ shop till you come to the ________________ box.
2. ________________ right at the ________________.
3. Go ________________ past the ________________ on your ________________.
4. ________________ the road at the cinema.
5. Then ________________ left at the next ________________.
6. The bank is on your ________________ on the other ________________ of the street.

Ü 5.4. Where's the station?

Write down the conversation. You (A) want to go to the station. Your partner (B) knows the way and helps you.

A: Sprich B an. Frage, ob er / sie dir den Weg zum Bahnhof sagen kann.

B: Bejahe dies und sage, dass A bis zum Ende der Straße geradeaus gehen muss und dann links.

A: Wiederhole die Anweisung und frage, ob das richtig war.

B: Bejahe dies und fahre fort mit der Anweisung. Sage, dass A weiter geradeaus gehen muss, bis er / sie ein Postamt erreicht. Dann die erste Straße links und die zweite rechts.

A: Frage, ob es weit ist.

B: Sage, dass A eine halbe Stunde braucht.

A: Reagiere enttäuscht. Frage, ob es einen Bus zum Bahnhof gibt.

B: Bejahe dies und sage, dass die Haltestelle dort drüben auf der anderen Straßenseite ist.

A: Bedanke dich.

AB: Verabschiedet euch.

6. Personal Pronouns

*Übungsziel:
Die persönlichen Fürwörter in verschiedenen Fällen kennen lernen*

Personal pronoun – subject and object

Jedes Substantiv / Nomen kann durch ein Personalpronomen ersetzt werden. Personalpronomen können als Subjekt oder als Objekt in Sätzen verwendet werden.

Wo ist Vater? — Er ist nicht im Wohnzimmer, ich habe ihn überall gesucht.

Er — ist das Personalpronomen für den Subjektfall.
Wer ist nicht im Wohnzimmer? → Er

ihn — ist das Personalpronomen für den Objektfall.
Wen habe ich gesucht? → ihn

Auch bei den englischen Personalpronomen unterscheidet man den
Ersatz für ein Subjekt → *subject*
Ersatz für ein Objekt → *object*

subject	predicate	object	
Mary	*sees*	*the boy.*	
She	*sees*	*him.*	
The busdriver	*knows*	*the girl.*	
He	*knows*	*her.*	
The children	*buy*	*presents.*	
They	*buy*	*them.*	

Forms of the personal pronoun – subject / object

Im Englischen gibt es für Substantive keine besondere Objektform. Bei den Pronomen muss man allerdings zwischen Subjekt- und Objektform unterscheiden.

Singular

first person

second person

third person

third person

third person

Plural

first person

second person

third person

Ü 6.1. Replacing

Replace the underlined words by the personal pronoun (object form).

1. You meet your teacher in the street.

You meet him in the street.

2. We have lunch with Peter and Sheila every day.

____.

3. He watches mother and me preparing breakfast.

____.

4. Put the cat outside.

____.

5. He puts his books on the bookshelf.

____.

6. Father drives his wife to town.

____.

7. She rides her bicycle to school every morning.

____.

8. Peggy calls father and me downstairs.

____.

9. You can go with Peter to the party.

____.

10. She puts the money in the bank.

____.

Ü 6.2. Eye-witnesses

Mary and Donald are looking out of the window onto the street. They are eye-witnesses of an accident. Put in the pronouns (object form).

eye-witness – Augenzeuge

Mary: Donald, look! The black car is turning into the main street. It hasn't got right of way.

Donald: Can you see that red car? The black car is crashing into it. Oh dear!

crash into – in … hineinfahren, hineinknallen

Mary: Oh, God. The driver of the black car – a woman – is lying on the street. Look! The policeman from the corner over there is running up to _________.

Donald: There's a big red bus. It has to stop in front of the two cars. That's lucky, it didn't run into _________.

run into – vgl. crash into

Mary: Look! The driver of the red car is getting out of his car. He's hurt. The policeman is turning to _________ and asking questions.

Donald: There's an old lady. Can you see _________? She's running to the phone box. But, look, she cannot open _________. The box is out of order.

Mary: Look! There's a dog running over to the policeman and the driver and the woman are lying on the ground. It is very excited and barking at _________.

Donald: Look over there! Kitty and Barbara and their friends are coming. Hey Kitty! We are up here! Can you see _________? Did you see the accident?

Kitty: Yes, we did.

Mary: Wait a minute, Kitty. We are coming down to _________ and we'll go to the policeman and tell _________ what we saw.

Übungsziel:
Mithilfe der Besitz anzeigenden Fürwörter Besitz ausdrücken

Personal pronouns – possessive form

Singular

I **my**

he **his**

you **your**

she **her**

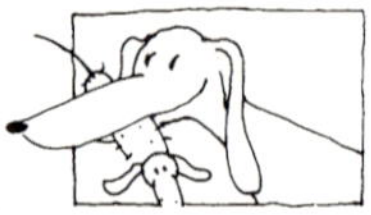
it **its**

Plural

we **our**

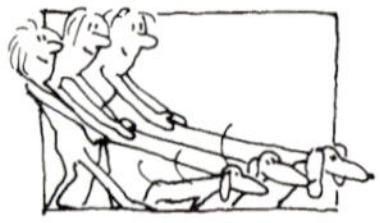
you **your**

they **their**

Ü 6.3. Filling in

Fill in the possessive pronouns.

		personal pronoun subject form	**possessive pronoun**	personal pronoun object form	Fill in
Singular	1st	I	my	me	This is my book.
	2nd	you	______	you	John, are you looking for ______ book?
	3rd	he	______	him	He often plays with ______ ball.
	3rd	she	______	her	She plays in ______ room.
	3rd	it	______	it	That is an old car. ______ windows are broken.
Plural	1st	we	______	us	We need new curtains for all ______ windows.
	2nd	you	______	you	Where have you put ______ socks?
	3rd	they	______	them	They are playing with ______ dolls.

Ü 6.4. Countries and languages

Put in the possessive pronouns and the languages.

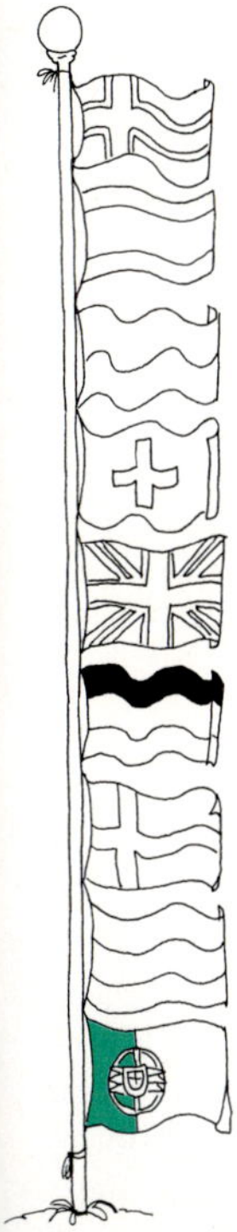

I come from Norway. My language is Norwegian.

I come from Spain. _______ language is _______________________.

We come from Poland. _______ language is ___________________.

He comes from Switzerland. _______ language is _______________.

She comes from Great Britain. _______ language is _____________.

You come from Germany. _______ language is _________________.

They come from Sweden. _______ language is _________________.

I come from Holland. _______ language is ____________________.

You come from Portugal. _______ language is __________________.

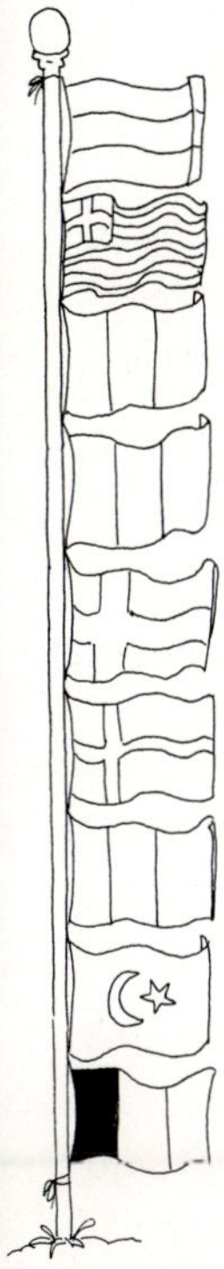

She comes from Austria. _______ language is __________________.

She comes from Greece. _______ language is __________________.

They come from France. _______ language is __________________.

I come from Ireland. _______ language is ____________________.

He comes from Finland. _______ language is ___________________.

We come from Denmark. _______ language is _________________.

We come from Italy. _______ language is ____________________.

He comes from Turkey. _______ language is ___________________.

She comes from Belgium. _______ language is _________________.

Ü 6.5. Moving in

move – umziehen

The Evans are moving into a new house. What do they need? Fill in the possessive pronouns and the names ot the rooms.

Mr. Evans: I need a new desk for my study.

Mrs. Evans: I need a new fridge for ________ ________.

Brenda / John: We need new curtains for ________ ________.

Mrs. Evans: No, not at all. The curtains are quite new. ________ colours are still nice and fresh. But we must have a new carpet in ________ sitting-room.

Mr. Evans: Brenda cannot sleep any longer in ________ old bed. She must have a new one.

Mrs. Evans: What about a new bookshelf? Do you need a new one in ________ room?

Brenda / John: Oh, yes, we'd like a new one. Thank you very much.

Mrs. Evans: John must also have a new lamp for ________ desk.

Mr. Evans: O. K. But now let's say hallo to ________ new neighbours. They are sitting in ________ garden and watching us.

Übungsziel: Die rückbezüglichen Fürwörter gebrauchen können

Reflexive pronoun

Das Reflexivpronomen (rückbezügliches Fürwort) wird verwendet, wenn Subjekt und Objekt dieselbe Person oder Sache bezeichnen.

Die Formen lauten: *myself, yourself, himself, herself, itself* und *ourselves, yourselves, themselves.*

Die Singularformen enden auf *-self*.
Die Pluralformen enden auf *-selves*.

Ü 6.6. Looking in a mirror

Fill in the reflexive pronoun.

When I look in a mirror I see myself________. 

you look you see ______________. 

he looks he sees ______________. 

she looks she sees ______________. 

it looks it sees ______________. 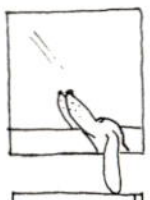

we look we see ______________. 

you look you see ______________. 

they look they see ______________. 

Ü 6.7. A strange party

Fill in the reflexive pronouns.

introduce – vorstellen

1. No one introduced me at the party, so I had to introduce ______________ to everyone.
2. No one gave us a drink at the party, so we had to help ______________.
3. No one showed us the way to the toilet, so we had to find it ______________.
4. The lady of the house played the piano very badly, she had taught ______________ how to play it.
5. Peter was not very careful when he cut the bread, so he cut ______________ with the knife.
6. The dog jumped onto a table full of things, when it saw ______________ in the mirror.

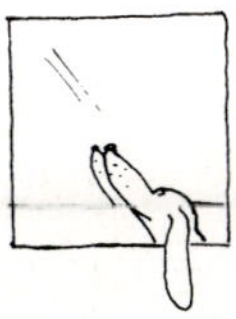

*Übungsziel:
Die Eigenschaften von Personen und Dingen ausdrücken und vergleichen können*

7. Adjectives

Eigenschaften und Merkmale von Personen, Lebewesen und Sachen werden durch Eigenschaftswörter (Adjektive) ausgedrückt. Die Adjektive stehen vor der Person, dem Lebewesen oder der Sache:

a pretty girl  *a quick dog* 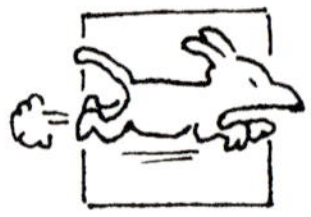 *an old school bag* 

oder nach dem Substantiv oder Pronomen und einer Form von *to be*:

the girl is pretty	*the dog is quick*	*the school bag is old*
she is pretty	*it is quick*	*it is old*

Die Form des Adjektivs bleibt immer unverändert.

Ü 7.1. Faces

Can you read the expressions on these faces? Match the adjectives. Choose from the words below.

*proud – stolz
confused – verwirrt
scared – ängstlich
ashamed – beschämt*

proud – confused – scared – happy – ashamed – tired – nervous – angry – ~~sad~~ – bored

Ü 7.2. Feelings

Look at the faces and write down how you feel. (You may also feel different from the suggestion!)

Deine Gefühle können auch anders sein als vorgeschlagen!

How do you feel when you …

1. are late for school: I feel ashamed.

2. get good marks in a test: ______________________.

3. think of holidays: ______________________.

4. someone kisses you: ______________________.

5. have a test: ______________________.

6. come to school: ______________________.

7. hear classical music: ______________________.

How do you feel when …

8. people talk about you: ______________________.

9. your friend doesn't talk to you: ______________________.

10. a teacher asks a question and you don't know the answer:

______________________.

Ü 7.3. What do you think?

Sage deine Meinung.

State your opinion. Make up sentences and write them down.

cheat – schwindeln

going to bed early		boring (langweilig)
doing tests		O. K. (in Ordnung)
watching TV		fascinating (faszinierend)
going to discos		not O. K.
learning English		good
getting back maths tests		silly (albern)
using make-up		nice (nett)
staying up late		lovely (angenehm)
doing the washing up	is	fantastic (fantastisch)
reading a book		exciting (aufregend)
riding a bike		clever (klug)
doing homework		helpful (hilfreich)
cheating in class		useful (nützlich)
cleaning your room		funny
having good friends		terrible (schrecklich)
doing sports		unneccessary (unnötig)
listening to music		stupid (dumm)

Example: Watching TV is fantastic.

Übungsziel: Adjektive steigern können

Comparisons: adjectives with *-er* and *-est*

Wenn du Vergleiche machen möchtest, musst du an ein Adjektiv *-er* oder *-est* anhängen.

John *Bob* *Richard*

tall *taller* *tallest*

John is tall. → **positive**
Bob is taller. → **comparative**
Richard is the tallest. → **superlative**

Mit *-er* und *-est* steigert man fast alle einsilbigen Adjektive.
Wichtige Ausnahme: *good – better – best.*
Genauso steigert man die zweisilbigen Adjektive, die auf *-y*, *-le*, *-er* oder *-ow* enden.

positive	comparative	superlative
young	*younger*	*the youngest*
small	*smaller*	*the smallest*
old	*older*	*the oldest*
simple	*simpler*	*the simplest*
happy	*happier*	*the happiest*
clever	*cleverer*	*the cleverest*
narrow	*narrower*	*the narrowest*

narrow – eng

1-silbige + *-y* / *-ow* **2-**silbige *-er* / *-le* Adjektive werden mit *-er* und *-est* gesteigert.

Ü 7.4. Correct order

Rewrite the words in correct order.

1. *Start with the youngest.*

a)	b)	c)
mother	father	grown-up
daughter	grandfather	baby
grandmother	son	teenager

grown-up – Erwachsener

Example: a) daughter, mother, grandmother

Auf der nächsten Seite geht es weiter!

2. *Start with the earliest.*

a)	b)	c)
Wednesday	tea	summer
Tuesday	dinner	spring
Sunday	breakfast	autumn

3. *Start with the smallest.*

matchbox car – Modell-auto

a)	b)	c)
house	horse	bus
hut	bird	matchbox car
skyscraper	elephant	taxi

Comparisons: adjectives with *more* and *most*

Alle anderen 2-silbigen Adjektive und die Adjektive mit 3 und mehr Silben werden mit *more* und *most* gesteigert.

positive	**comparative**	**superlative**
boring 	*more boring* 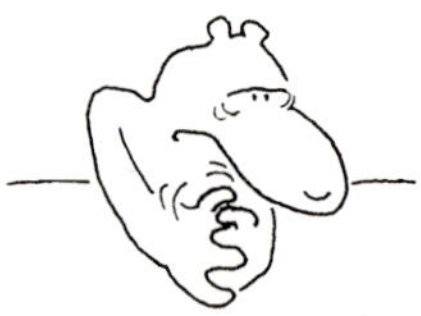	*the most boring* 
modern	*more modern*	*the most modern*
beautiful	*more beautiful*	*the most beautiful*
interesting	*more interesting*	*the most interesting*

Ü 7.5. How many syllables?

Write the adjectives below in the right boxes.

syllable – Silbe

one syllable	two syllables ending in -y, -er, -le, -ow	two syllables	three or more syllables
fat	funny	tired	intelligent

thin – ~~tired~~ – uncomfortable – easy – narrow – fascinating – terrible – ~~fat~~ – noble – happy – beautiful – ~~funny~~ – simple – clever – wonderful – modern – crazy – old – ~~intelligent~~ – tall – nice – noisy – loud

uncomfortable – unbequem

Rules of writing

- Ein stummes *-e* am Ende des Adjektivs fällt bei der Steigerung weg:

  simple – simpler – the simplest

- Ein Konsonant, der nach einem kurzen Vokal steht, wird bei der Steigerung verdoppelt:

  hot – hotter – the hottest

- nach einem Mitlaut wird *-y* zu *-i*:

  happy – happier – the happiest

Ü 7.6. Comparatives and superlatives

Fill in the missing forms.

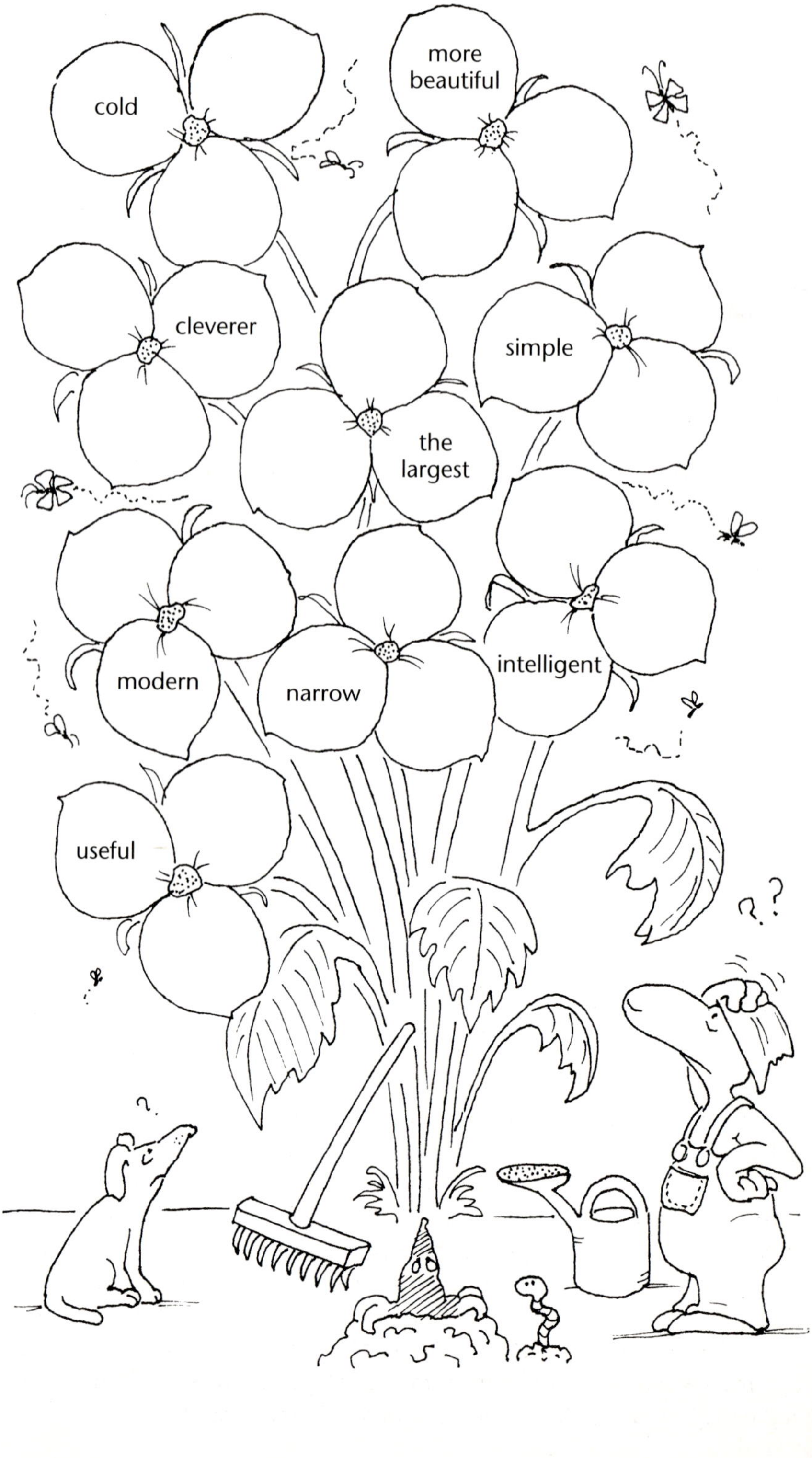

Ü 7.7. Comparing persons and things

Look at the pictures. Write sentences in your exercise book.

1. tall

2. expensive

3. fast

4. strong

5. exciting

6. beautiful

Example:

1. Fred is tall. His brother in the middle is taller. His father is the tallest.

Ü 7.8. My class

Peter tells something about his class and his teachers. Read the text and mark the adjectives.

In my class there are 26 pupils, 12 boys and 14 girls. Sarah is our sweetest girl. She looks very pretty with her blue eyes and fair hair. The smallest girl is Betty but she is not the youngest. She is one year older than the others. The tallest girl is Helen. She is very good at running. Peter is the best looking boy in our class. He is also the nicest one. Pamela likes him very much. Daniel is the most intelligent boy. He is good at most school subjects. Our history teacher is the funniest woman. Her voice is loud and she talks too fast and too much. She is the fastest speaker. Our maths lessons aren't very interesting. Our teacher walks into the classroom and tells us to open our maths books and do the exercises. That is the most boring lesson in school.

Now talk about the people in your class. Use the adjectives below.

Who is the	strong – good looking – sweet – funny – loud – intelligent – fast – slow – beautiful – nice – noisy – awful	?

The strongest girl in our class is …

Irregular comparisons

Manche Adjektive haben unregelmäßige Steigerungsformen. Du lernst sie am besten auswendig.

These marks are **good**.

These marks are **better**.

These are **the best** *marks.*

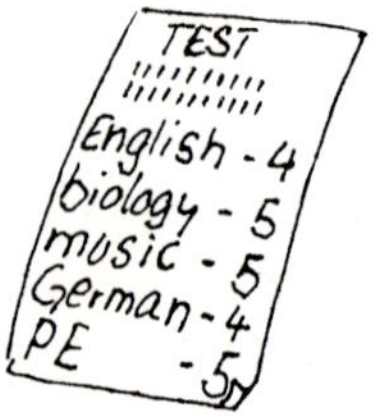

These marks are **bad**.

These marks are **worse**.

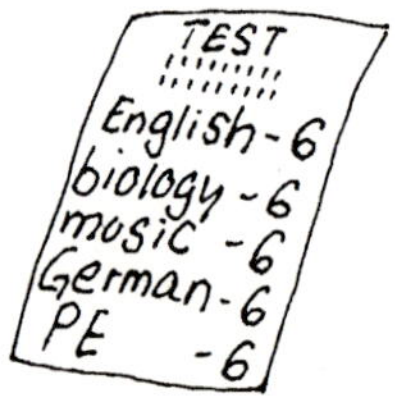

These are **the worst**.

Tom is **little**.

Mary is **smaller**.

Peter is the **smallest**.

John doesn't have **much** *money.*

Tom has **more** *money.*

Jerry has **the most** *money.*

positive	comparative	superlative
good	*better*	*the best*
bad	*worse*	*the worst*
little	*smaller*	*the smallest*
much *many*	*more*	*the most*

Ü 7.9. Using irregular comparisons

Fill in the right forms.

1. You drink too ______________ coke. You drink ______________ than me.
2. I had ______________ mistakes in my maths test. My friend had ______________. But Helen had ______________.
3. I have got a little pet. It's a dog. But there are ______________ pets. A cat is ______________ and a budgie is ______________.
4. *Compare the school reports.*
   Use bad – worse – worst / good – better – best

a) Mabel is ______________ at English, but Helen is ______________.

b) Mabel is ______________ at German, too. Peter is ______________ but Helen is ______________.

c) Peter is ______________ at biology, but Helen is even ______________ and Mabel is ______________.

Comparisons in sentences

Personen und Dinge können mithilfe von Adjektiven und der Wendung *as … as* verglichen werden, wenn man die Gleichheit beschreiben will.

Betont man die Unterschiede, dann verwendet man die Wendung *not as … as*.

Man kann auch die Steigerungsform eines Adjektivs und die Wendung *than* verwenden.

Verwechsle nicht das Wort *than* = als mit *then* = denn / dann.

My father is as old as my mother. They are both 38 years old.

My sister is not as old as my brother. She is 8 years old. My brother is 10 years old.

My grandfather is older than my grandmother. He is 65 years old and she is only 55.

Ü 7.10. Lines and squares

square – Rechteck

Compare the lines.

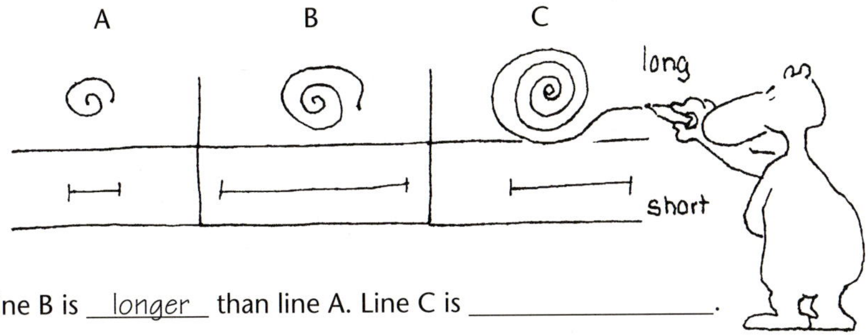

1. Line B is longer than line A. Line C is ______________.

   Line B is not so ______________ as line C.

2. Line B is ____

   ____.

Compare the squares and answer the questions below.

1. Is the pale green square the widest? No, the striped square is the widest.
2. Is the white square the narrowest? ______________________.
3. Is the striped square the longest? ______________________.
4. Is the grey square 1 cm wide? ______________________.
5. Is the white square 2 cm wider than the green square?

   ____.
6. Which square is narrower than the white square?

   ____.
7. Which square is as wide as the grey square? ______________________.
8. Which square is 1 cm wider than the green square?

   ____.
9. Which square is longer than the striped square? ______________________.
10. Which square is the widest? ______________________.

Ü 7.11. Free time activities

Compare the activities and write down in your exercise book what you think about them. Use nice – interesting – expensive – difficult – good – hard – easy

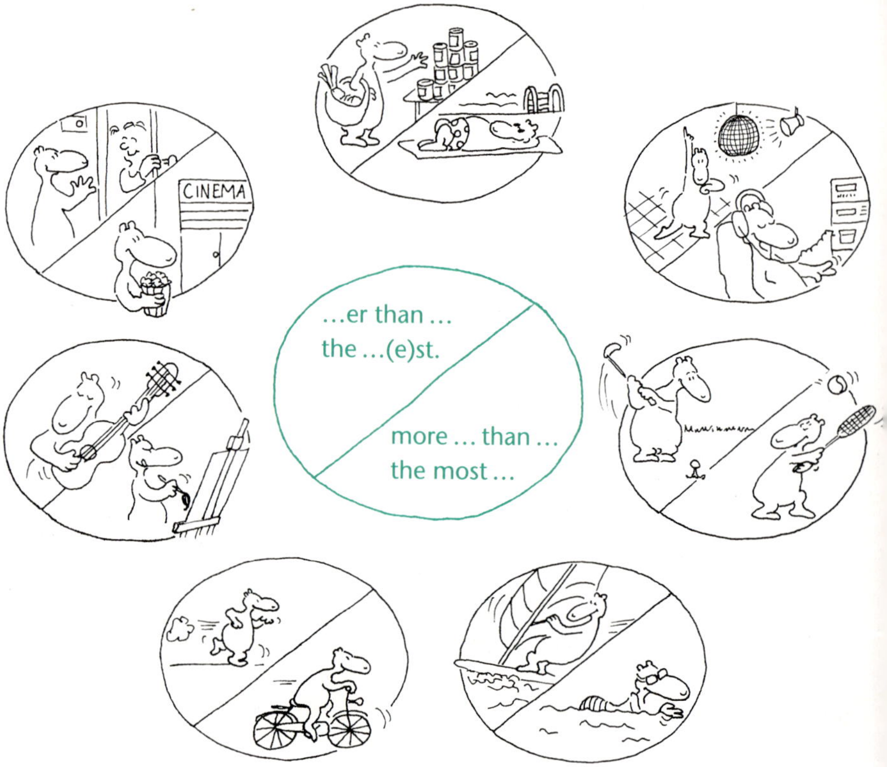

Example: Lying in the sun is nicer than going shopping.

Now over to you. Talk about yourself. You can use the words below as a help.

1. Most of my pocket money goes for …
2. I think … is more exciting than …
3. I need … much more than …
4. Most of my teachers are …
5. To me … is more important than …
6. Most of my friends are …
7. I spend more time on … than on …
8. The funniest picture I saw was …
9. The most exciting book I read was …
10. My friend likes … more than …
11. For me … is more useful than …
12. I need my bike as much as …

radio – classical music – swimming – friends – listening to CDs – speaking English – video games – milk – football – coffee – tea – school – watching TV – my radio – homework – reading – skateboard

Ü 7.12. Comparing pets

Fill in the names of the pets and the right forms of the adjectives.

Peggy has got a  _______________. She thinks her _______________ is _______________ (nice) than Pat's  _______________. But Pat thinks that her _______________ is ____________________ (beautiful) than Peggy's _______________.

Dick's pet is a  _______________. It is one of the _______________ (quiet) pets he knows. His sister's  _______________ is _______________ (noisy) than his _______________.

Mr. Brown loves to watch his  _______________. Every day he tells his wife that his _______________ are _________________ (interesting) pets he knows.

Mrs. Brown doesn't love her husband's __________________ very much. She thinks her  ______ is ________ (interesting) than his _______________.

Brenda has got a  ____________________ with long white hair. It is _________________ (beautiful) than the other _______________ in the street.

Peter doesn't like ___________. He thinks they are ___________ (stinky) pets he knows. Peter has got a  _______________. It is _______________ (big) than Richard's poodle Joey, but Joey is ________________ (intelligent) than Peter's _______________.

Sally has not got a pet. But her favourite animal is a  _______________, because _______________ are _______________ (intelligent) pets she knows. Sally thinks _______________ are _______________ (lovely and funny) pets.

budgie – goldfish – canary – monkey – dog – rabbit – guinea-pig – cat

Übungsziel:
Das britische Schulsystem kennen lernen.

8. British Schools

A pupil in Britain has a long school day. School starts at nine o'clock – that's nice! – but it ends about four o'clock in the afternoon – that's a very long day.

lesson – Unterrichtsstunde
assembly – Morgenversammlung
important events – wichtige Angelegenheiten
hymn – feierlicher Gesang
prayer – Gebet

assembly

In the morning before lessons start all teachers and pupils meet in the assembly hall. The headmaster tells everyone about important events at school. Usually someone plays the piano and the pupils sing hymns, and the teachers say prayers.

classroom

After that the pupils go to the classrooms. Each teacher has his own classroom that he always teaches in. When the bell rings at the end of the lesson, the teachers stay in their classrooms and the pupils have to go to them. Some of the classrooms look very interesting because a lot of teachers have pictures and sometimes even models about what they teach in their classrooms.

meals

School is open all day, and so the pupils stay there for lunch. Teachers and pupils usually eat together in the cafeteria. Pupils can buy lunch in the cafeteria or bring sandwiches from home.

library

There are a lot of activities for pupils at lunchtime. For example they can go to a drama club or play or read in the library in bad weather.

court – Spielfeld

sports

The school is closed on Saturdays. But there are often matches against other schools then. Many schools have their own swimming pool and there are also courts for tennis and playing fields for football, hockey and cricket.

Ü 8.1. Right or wrong?

Rewrite the sentences that are wrong.

	+	–
1. Every morning starts with lunch where all the pupils eat together.		
2. The pupils have to go to the teacher's classrooms.		
3. When it rains pupils must go outside.		
4. There are lessons on Saturdays.		
5. All pupils go home for lunch.		
6. There are a lot of sports matches between different schools.		
7. At four o'clock must pupils go to the swimming-pool.		
8. Pupils have six days school a week.		
9. Sport is an important part of school life.		
10. Pupils can't play with their friends in the afternoons.		

Ü 8.2. Susan's day

Susan writes a letter about a typical school-day in Britain.
Read her letter and rewrite the letter in your exercise book. Replace the pictures by words.

Dear Peter,

Everyday I  at . I usually leave home at . I ride my  to school every day. The journey takes me  an hour. School starts at . After  go to Mr. Walker's classroom. My first lesson is maths. It starts at . At  we have a break. Every morning my class have a  break from  to .  is lunchtime.

break – Pause

We all go to the  and have lunch there with our . My favourite menu is , 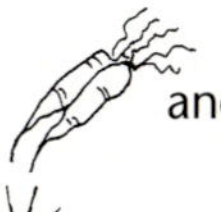 and . In  I go to the  and read . If the  shines I go to the playground and play  In the afternoon lessons go on. At  I get my  from the shed and hurry home. Then I do homework or play with friends.

In the evening I watch . At  I go to 

yours Susan.

assembly – books – sun – bed – carrots – library – TV – hamburgers – teachers – pears – football – bad weather – bike – get up – cafeteria

Ü 8.3. Your school day

Answer the questions.

1. When do you get up? I get up at ________ in the morning.

tick – ankreuzen

2. How do you get to school? Tick I ______________________________.
   ☐ I walk ☐ I cycle
   ☐ I go by bus ☐ I go by train ☐ I go by car
3. When do you usually arrive at school? ______________________________.
4. At what time does school start in the morning? ______________________________.
5. How many breaks do you have? ______________________________.
6. At what time does school finish? ______________________________.
7. Where do you eat lunch? ______________________________.
8. When do you go home? ______________________________.
9. Where and when do you do your homework? ______________________________.

Now write about one day at school.

In the morning I get up at ____________. I go to school ____________ and arrive there at ____________. The first break is at ____________. Then ____________. School finishes at ____________. I go ____________.

Ü 8.4. An ideal school

This is what English pupils say about their dream school.

"I'd like the teacher to use more films and television and cassette recordings in class. I go to sleep if I have to look at the blackboard all the time." **Benny (12)**

gymnasium – Turnhalle

"I'd like to use all the school sports facilities in the holidays. In an ideal school I'd like a swimming pool, a gymnasium, a football field, squash courts and tennis courts." **Peter (13)**

"I'd like more clubs – drama clubs, photography clubs, film clubs. We've already got these clubs in our school – but they're all for the older pupils." **Penny (11)**

less – weniger

"I'd like more holidays, and less homework, and no tests." **Rick (12)**

"I'd like very small classes – not more than twenty pupils in a class. In a big class, you put up your hand to answer a question, but the teacher never sees you." **Sue (13)**

Your ideal school

What would your ideal school be like?
Write a short text.
Use the words to help you.
I'd like more …
In an ideal school there would be …

I'd like	more	films.
	less	TV.
	smaller	holidays.
		homework.
		cassette recordings.
		videos.
		classes
		…

Ü 8.5. Your school

Write about your school.

In my class there are … pupils.
the schoolbooks are boring
My English teacher is …
My school is called …
not very interesting
too many tests
modern classrooms
My favourite teacher is …
too many pupils in the classroom
some teachers are O. K. … I am in form …
good teachers … too small … too big … too noisy … My form teacher is …

favourite teacher – Lieblingslehrer

pupils: There are about ______________________________.

classes: ______________________________.

teachers: ______________________________.

classrooms: ______________________________.

course rooms: ______________________________.

other rooms/places: ______________________________.

course – Kurs, Arbeitsgemeinschaft

What I think about

our classroom: ______________________________.

the teachers: ______________________________.

homework: ______________________________.

I would like to have (more): ______________________________

______________________________.

I wish we had less: ______________________________.

Übungsziel: Die Namen der Schulfächer kennen lernen.

Ü 8.6. School subjects

Which number goes with which subject?
Fill in the subject.

1. German

2. ____________

3. ____________

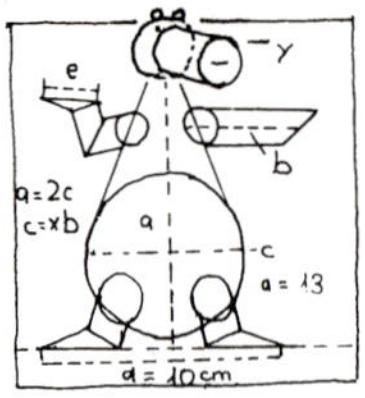

4. ____________

5. ____________

6. ____________

7. science

8. ____________

9. ____________

10. ____________

11. ____________

12. religious education (R.E.)

13. ____________

14. ____________

15. ____________

science – Naturwissenschaft(en)

cookery / domestic science – physical education (P.E.) – needlework – German – biology – science – music – art – mathematics (maths) – geography – drama – woodwork – history – English – religious education (R.E.)

Ü 8.7. Interview with Tony about his favourite subject

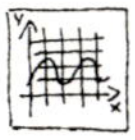

Fred: Tony, what's your favourite subject?
Tony: I like P.E. very much because I like running and jumping.
Fred: How many P.E. lessons do you have?
Tony: We have three P.E. lessons every week. It's not boring. Some subjects are boring. Maths is boring.
Fred: You like English too, don't you?
Tony: Yes, I do, we all like English lessons.
Fred: Why?
Tony: Because Mrs Woolworth is a good teacher. She's very friendly. We play a lot of games in English lessons – shopping games and word games.
Fred: Thank you for the interview.

favourite subject, lesson – Lieblingsfach
boring – langweilig

What do you think about your subjects?

Write in your exercise book.

English

P.E.
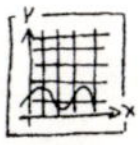
maths

geography

music

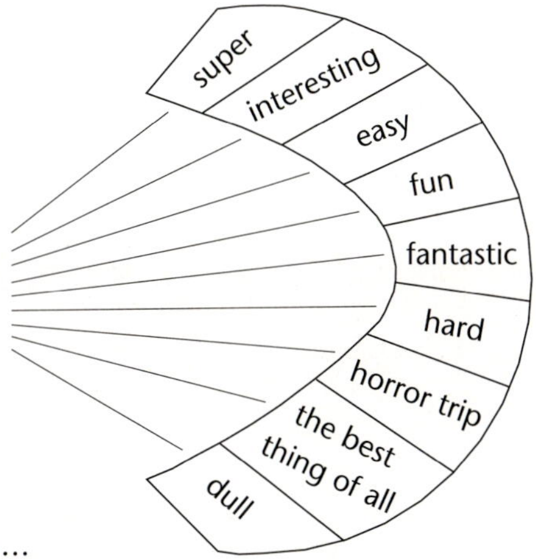

English is super. P.E. is ...

dull – langweilig

Ü 8.8. Your school report

Now you can write your own school report. Fill in the blanks from the list of words and choose subjects.

school report – Schulzeugnis

SCHOOL REPORT

Name of Student ________________________
(write your name here)

I'm ________________ at ________________.

I'm ________________ at ________________.

I'm ________________ at ________________.

I'm ________________ at ________________.

I'm ________________ at ________________.

good – bad – awful – lazy – brilliant – slow – forgetful – the best – quick – the worst

awful – furchtbar
lazy – faul
brilliant – ausgezeichnet
the worst – der Schlechteste

Ü 8.9. A timetable

School: Kingstown
Class: 2 B
Teacher: Mr. Evans

SCHOOL TIMETABLE

Name:
Benny Woodwell

P.E.

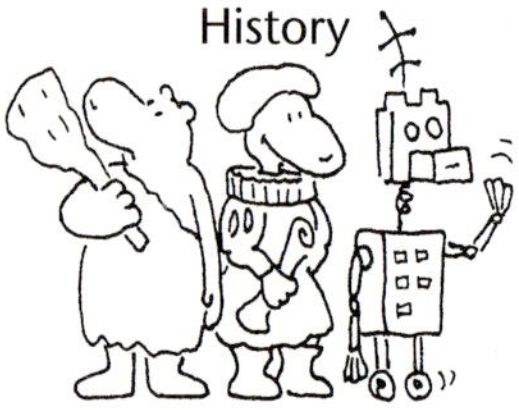
History

Drama

English

Music

Maths

German

Science

Time	Mon	Tues	Wed	Thurs	Fri
9.00	Assembly				
9.20					
10.00					
10.40	Morning Break				
11.00					
12.00					
12.40	Dinner Break				
2.00					
2.40				Cookery Woodwork	Cookery Woodwork
3.20				Swimming	
4.00		Drama		Swimming	Film Club

Geography

Art

Cookery

Woodwork

Read the sentences and write the subjects in the correct places in the timetable.

1. After the morning break on Monday we have maths and before the morning break we have P.E.
2. The first lesson on Monday is German.
3. The first lesson on Wednesday is the same as on Monday.
4. After German on Monday we have physical education.
5. The fifth lesson on Monday is art.
6. The last lesson on Wednesday is biology.
7. We have a double English lesson before morning break on Tuesday.
8. We don't have P.E. on Wednesday.
9. The first lesson after dinner break on Thursday ist R.E.

10. On Wednesday afternoon we have maths before art and needlework before biology.
11. We have music on Friday morning.
12. Dinner break is after art on Wednesday.
13. We have two art lessons on Wednesday.
14. Science is the second lesson on Thursday.
15. There are two science lessons on Thursday. The second science lesson starts after morning break.
16. The last two lessons on Monday are English and P.E.
17. Between history and geography in the afternoon on Tuesday is biology.
18. Before drama on Tuesday is geography.
19. Thursday starts with maths and ends with swimming.
20. After science on Friday is morning break.
21. The last lesson before dinner break on Thursday is music.
22. Biology is before dinner break on Friday and history is after dinner break.
23. The third and fourth lessons before dinner break on Tuesday are maths and P.E.
24. The fifth lesson on Tuesday is the same as the fifth lesson on Friday.
25. The second lesson on Wednesday is the same as the second lesson on Tuesday.
26. Between art and English in the afternoon on Monday is music.
27. The fourth lesson on Monday is religious education.
28. On Friday we have German before the film club.
29. We have the same lesson after morning break on Friday as after morning break on Tuesday.
30. The first lesson after morning break on Wednesday is geography.

Übungsziel:
Zeitwörter und ihre Bedeutung kennen lernen

9. Verbs

Die wichtigsten Wörter in einer Fremdsprache sind die Verben. Je mehr Verben du kennst, umso besser kannst du dich ausdrücken.
Verben bezeichnen meist eine Tätigkeit, manchmal auch einen Zustand.

Ü 9.1. Fred and his jobs

Read the list of verbs and fill in the missing letters under the pictures.

to eat *to sleep*	essen schlafen
to rest	ruhen
to live	leben
to stand up *to lie (down)* *to get up*	aufstehen sich hinlegen aufstehen
to clean *to wash* *to brush*	säubern waschen bürsten
to build	bauen

to drink *to wake up*	trinken aufwachen
to polish *to wipe*	polieren wischen
to stay	wohnen
to sit (down) *to fall*	sich hinsetzen fallen
to work *to play*	arbeiten spielen
to dig	graben

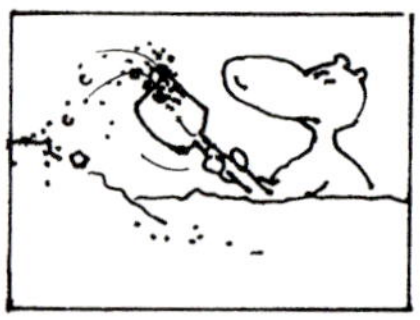
to d . .

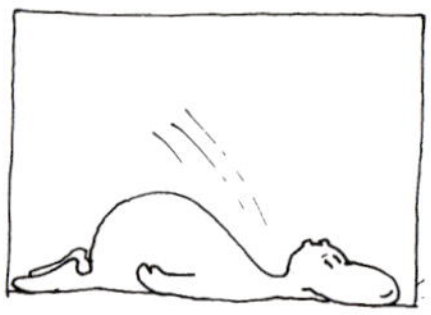
to l . .

to cl . . n

to d . i . .

to w . s .

to w . p .

to w . k . . p

to w . . k

to l . . e

to s . . nd u .

to . l . . p

to b . . sh

to . . . d . . n

to g . t u .

to r . s .

to p . l . s .

to throw *to drop*	werfen fallen lassen
to start *to finish*	anfangen beenden
to go *to stop*	gehen halten
to fetch *to carry*	holen tragen
to keep	behalten
to break *to tear*	brechen reißen
to give *to lend*	geben (ver)leihen

to catch *to pick up*	fangen aufsammeln
to begin *to go on* *to stop*	beginnen weitermachen anhalten
to come *to wait*	kommen warten
to bring *to take*	(mit-, her)bringen hinbringen
to give back	zurückgeben
to cut *to burn*	schneiden brennen
to send *to get*	schicken bekommen

to c . t

to b . . n

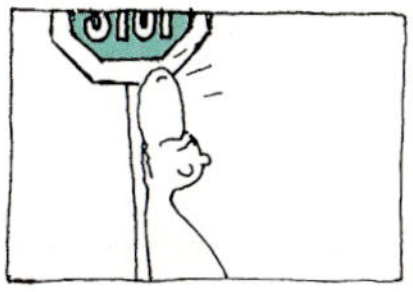

to s . . .

to . ai .

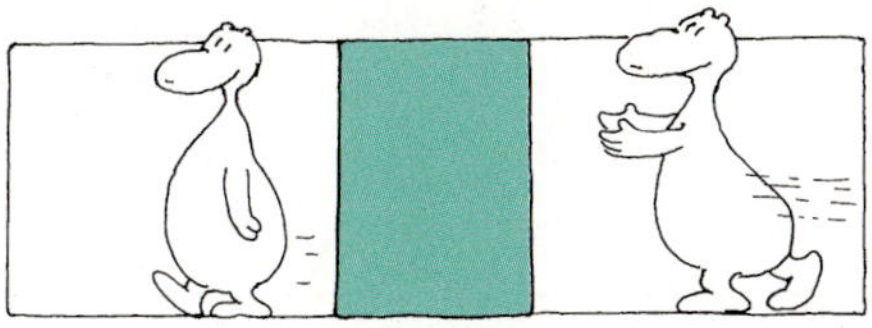

to . o

to c . m .

to b . . n .

to l . . d

to t . . r

to s . . d

to g . t

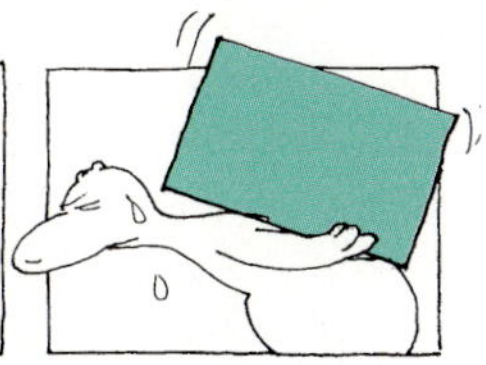

to . ar . y

to g . . .

to g . v . b . . k

to b . . . k

to p . . k u .

i

to climb *to ride* *to pass*	klettern reiten vorbeifahren, vorbeigehen …
to swim *to fly*	schwimmen fliegen
to fight *to hurt*	kämpfen verletzen
to rain	regnen
to hide *to find*	verstecken finden

to creep *to drive*	kriechen fahren
to sink	sinken
to shoot *to kick*	schießen schießen (Fußball)
to shine	scheinen (Sonne)
to lose	verlieren

to . r . . .

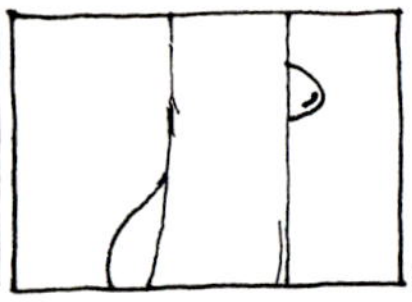
to h . d .

to s . . n .

to . . rt

to . . de

to . w . m

to f . g . t

to k . ck

to c . ee .

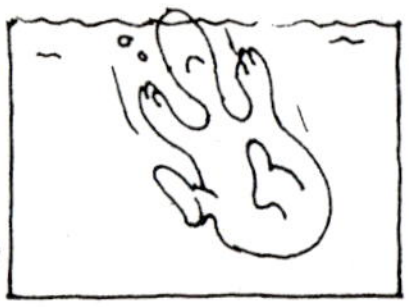
to s . . k

to p . . s

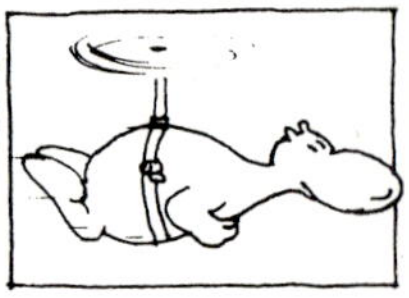
to . l .

to s . . . t

to c . i . b

to . ai .

to l . s .

to . . nd

to think *to expect*	denken erwarten
to hear *to taste*	hören schmecken
to point at …	auf … zeigen
to read *to draw*	lesen zeichnen
to say *to ask* *to call*	sagen fragen rufen
to teach	lehren
to know *to remember*	wissen erinnern

to believe *to hope*	glauben hoffen
to see *to listen (to)*	sehen zuhören
to look at *to show*	ansehen zeigen
to write	schreiben
to speak *to tell* *to answer*	sprechen erzählen antworten
to learn	lernen
to understand *to forget*	verstehen vergessen

to l . a . .

to . x . . c .

to t . . n .

to . as . .

to unde . st . . d

to k . . w

to . . y

to . r . w

to p . . n . (at)

to . . e

to r . . em . . .

to . s .

to . ea .

to f . rg . .

to . . . ch

to b . . i . v .

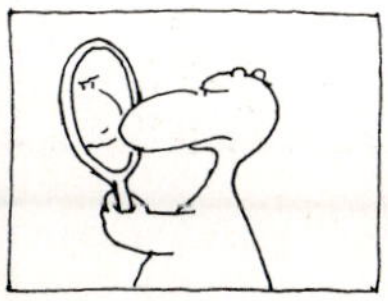
to l . . k

to . . . l

to . . p .

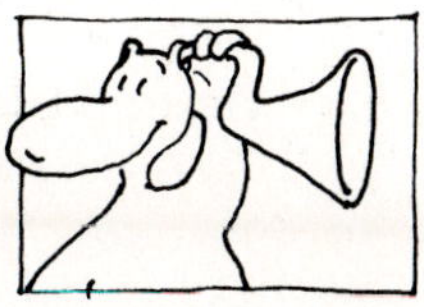
to l . . t . n (t .)

to help *to meet*	helfen treffen	*to follow*	folgen
to use *to exchange*	gebrauchen tauschen	*to wear*	tragen
to buy *to pay*	kaufen bezahlen	*to sell* *to steal*	verkaufen stehlen

to u . .

to w . . r

to f . ll . w

to . ay

to exch . . ge

to m . . t

to . e . p

to s . e . l

Ü 9.2. Verbs and nouns

Match the nouns to the verbs and write down the sentences.

1	We eat	evening	A
2	We drink	horses	B
3	We pick	cameras	C
4	We ask and answer	beds	D
5	We write with	milk	E
6	We see films in	bookshop	F
7	We sleep in	school	G
8	We tell	questions	H
9	We ride on	pencils	I
10	We drive	bus	J
11	We hear with our	eyes	K
12	We speak with our	ears	L
13	We cut bread with	stories	M
14	We wear	sandwiches	N
15	We take photos with	flowers	O
16	We go to school by	jeans	P
17	We learn English at	cinemas	Q
18	We buy books at the	cars	R
19	We watch TV every	knives	S
20	We see with our	mouths	T

Example: 1 N *We eat sandwiches.*

False friends

Es gibt eine Reihe von Verben im Englischen, die eine andere Bedeutung haben, als du im Deutschen vermuten würdest. Man nennt sie *false friends*.

make herstellen / anfertigen / machen

Mother makes a cake: Mutter stellt einen Kuchen her (backt einen Kuchen).

do 1. tun / verrichten
2. in Ordnung bringen / erledigen

1. *What are you doing?:* Was tust (machst) du gerade?
2. *Peter does his homework:* Peter erledigt seine Hausaufgaben.

Ü 9.3. Matching exercise: *make – do*

Match the right pairs and learn the phrases by heart.

to make

1	a coat	A	einen Mantel schneidern
2	a speech	B	Fratzen schneiden
3	plans	C	eine Rede halten
4	a mistake	D	Krach machen
5	money	E	Pläne machen
6	faces	F	einen Fehler machen
7	a fire	G	telefonieren
8	the bed	H	Geld verdienen
9	a noise	I	das Bett machen
10	a telephone call	J	Feuer anzünden

1	A
2	
3	
4	
5	
6	
7	
8	
9	
10	

to do

1	one's best	A	rechnen
2	the washing-up	B	seine Hausaufgaben machen
3	a test	C	60 Meilen schnell fahren
4	right	D	richtig handeln
5	one's homework	E	das Zimmer aufräumen
6	somebody a favour	F	einen Test schreiben
7	wrong	G	abwaschen
8	the room	H	sein Bestes tun
9	60 miles an hour	I	jemanden einen Gefallen tun
10	sums	J	falsch handeln

1	
2	
3	
4	
5	
6	
7	
8	
9	
10	

Ü 9.4. What a life!

Put in the missing forms of do or make.

First Mother has breakfast. Then she ______________ the rooms and ______________ the beds. Later she ______________ a little gardening. After that she ______________ the shopping. When she comes back, she ______________ herself a cup of tea and begins to prepare the dinner. When Peter is back from school he ______________ his homework. After supper they all ______________ the dishes. Mother likes homemade cake, so she usually ______________ a cake for the weekend.

homemade cake – selbst gebackener Kuchen

Ü 9.5. A dialogue

Fill in: do / make or doing / making.

Susan (calling from downstairs): Peter, what are you doing? ______________

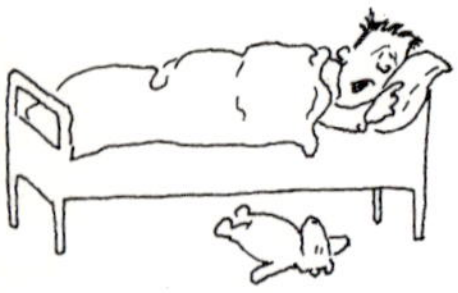

Peter: I'm ______________ my bed.

Susan: But I thought you wanted to ______________ a phone call to Mum in hospital?

Peter: All right. I'll ______________ that in a minute.

Susan: And tomorrow you are going to ______________ a test. So you have to ______________ some work for school.

Peter: O.K. But I haven't got much time to ______________ it now. I still have a lot of things to ______________. I've got to help Dad first.

Ü 9.6. What you *make* and what you *do*

Write in your exercise book.

the beds – my homework – breakfast – the washing-up – a fire – right – coffee – a test – my best – a noise – a mistake – a telephone call – wrong – the room

I do …	I make …
my homework	the beds

take – bring

to take kennzeichnet immer eine Bewegung vom Sprecher weg:
hinbringen – wegbringen

Take the letter to the post office.
Bring den Brief zum Postamt.

to bring kennzeichnet immer eine Bewegung zum Sprecher hin:
herbringen – mitbringen

Bring me the letter.
Bring mir den Brief her.

Ü 9.7. Family help

taking to ⟶ a place
bringing back from ⟵

You ask your father what you have to do in the household. He answers:

a piece of soap	bathroom	some stamps
cups	kitchen	some towels
tools	your room	Betty's sandals
magazines	shoemaker's	Father's hammer
parcels	neighbour	the vacuum cleaner
papers	post office	your schoolbag
shirts	cellar	some black shoe polish
black shoes	to Betty's room	some postcards

Example: Take the parcels to the post office and bring back some post-cards.

Verbs of hearing

to hear bedeutet „hören ohne Absicht".
to listen (to) heißt „(jemandem) bewusst zuhören / lauschen".

Ü 9.8. Filling in

Fill in the gaps.

1. Don't ______________ her, she is a silly goose.
2. We can't ______________ what he is saying.
3. I ______________ a noise.
4. We ______________ but ______________ nothing.

silly goose – dumme Gans

Verbs of seeing

to see bedeutet „sehen“ im Sinne von „ungewollt wahrnehmen“.
to look meint „bewusst nach etwas schauen“.
to watch heißt „beobachten“ oder „anschauen“.

Ü 9.9. Filling in

Fill in the gaps.

1. Blind people cannot _______________.
2. The little girl was _______________ at the dolls.
3. Every night father and mother _______________ TV.
4. What can you _____________ when you _____________ out of the window?

Ü 9.10. Verbs of looking / seeing and hearing

Fill in the suitable verbs of looking, seeing and hearing.

1. He ____hears____ them talking, but doesn't __understand__ what they are ____saying____.
2. When he walks through the park, he _______________ a bird sing.
3. The little girl has to _______________ over the shoulders of the man in front of her to _______________ the match.
4. Mother really _______________ everywhere but she can't find the purse.
5. He quickly _______________ over the page.
6. You can't _______________ in the dark.
7. Father _________________ up from his book and ___________________ his brother Jim, whom he has not _______________ for years.
8. The boy _______________ at the old lady's funny dress.
9. When they _______________ the noise, they all _______________.

purse – Geldbeutel

The verbs *become* and *get*

to become heißt „werden“ ganz allgemein.
to get bedeutet „bekommen / erhalten“.

Ü 9.11. *become* and *get*

Fill in the gaps.

1. You can _______________ apples at the greengrocer's.
2. He has _______________ a teacher.

3. Mother was very angry when she could not _____________ a taxi.

4. My sister wants to _____________ President when she is big.

5. How much pocket money do you _____________?

6. Queen Elizabeth II. _____________ Queen of England in 1952.
(past tense!)

Ü 9.12. Can you become a beefsteak?

Read the story, look at the picture and answer the questions.

A young German has travelled to London by train. He gets off the train at Victoria Station. It has been a long journey and the young German feels very hungry. He goes to a restaurant to get something to eat. It is lunchtime and all the restaurants are full. But then he finds an empty seat in one of them. The waiters hurry from table to table to serve the guests. When one of the waiters comes to his table, the German orders a beefsteak. He has to wait a long time for his meal. Half an hour passes – no beefsteak. The young man becomes hungrier and hungrier. When an hour has passed, he shouts in a loud voice: "Waiter, when shall I become a beefsteak?" "Never, I hope, sir," is the waiter's answer.

waiter – Ober, Kellner

pass – hier: verstreichen

1. Where does the German travel to? He travels to London.

2. Where does he get off the train?

____.

3. Why does he go to a restaurant?

____.

4. What does the German order in the restaurant?

____.

5. How does he shout?

____.

6. What does he shout?

____.

7. What does the waiter answer?

____.

8. Can you become a beefsteak?

____.

*Übungsziel:
Die unvollständigen Hilfsverben gebrauchen können*

10. Defective Auxiliaries

Unvollständige Hilfsverben heißen deshalb unvollständig, weil sie nicht alle Zeiten bilden können.

Sie werden nur in Verbindung mit Vollverben verwendet und informieren uns im Allgemeinen darüber, **wie** etwas getan wird. Es ist z. B. ein großer Unterschied, ob ich schwimmen kann, darf, will, muss …!

I can speak English

can – cannot – can't (nicht) können	drückt geistige und körperliche Fähigkeit aus: *I can swim.* *He can speak English but he cannot / can't speak French.*
could – couldn't konnten (nicht) könnten (nicht)	• ist die Vergangenheitsform von *can*: *He could speak French very well but now he is out of practise.* • wird als höfliche Frage benutzt: *Could you help me please?*
must müssen	drückt ein notwendiges Müssen aus: *You must learn your English words.*
mustn't nicht dürfen	drückt ein Verbot aus: *You mustn't talk so much.*
need brauchen … zu	drückt Notwendigkeit aus: *Need I tell you more?*
needn't nicht brauchen	drückt die Verneinung der Notwendigkeit aus: *You needn't work so hard.*

may / may not (nicht) dürfen	drückt eine Erlaubnis aus: *May I go out? Yes, you may.*
will / would wollen / würden	drücken eine Bitte oder einen Wunsch aus: *Will / Would you help me, please?*

Unvollständige Hilfsverben

haben kein *-s* in der 3. Person Singular der Gegenwart:	*He can swim.* *She mustn't come in.*
werden in Frage und Verneinung nicht mit *to do* umschrieben (wie die Vollverben):	*May I go out?* *You cannot fly.*
haben den Infinitiv eines Vollverbs (ohne *to*) nach sich:	*She can speak English.* *We may go.*

Can – can't – could – couldn't

Folgende Formen sind wichtig:

+	*can*	*could*	*could*
–	*cannot / can't*	*couldn't*	*couldn't*
	present	**past**	**conditional**

Ü 10.1. Animals

Describe what the animals can do or can't do. Write in your exercise book.

fly – swim – run fast – jump – hear well – pull cars – climb trees – sing – see well – smell very well – catch mice – eat other animals – live without water – eat bananas – bark

Example: A rabbit can run very fast but it can't see very well.

Ü 10.2. Spare time activities

Match the activities below to the pictures. Write under the pictures.

1 ____________________

2 ____________________

3 ____________________

4 ____________________

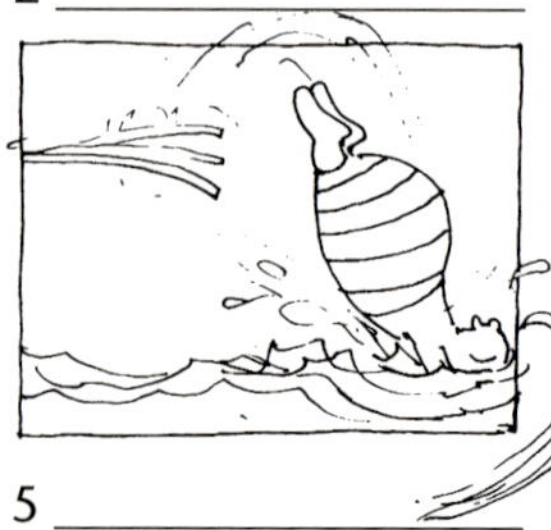

5 ____________________

6 ____________________

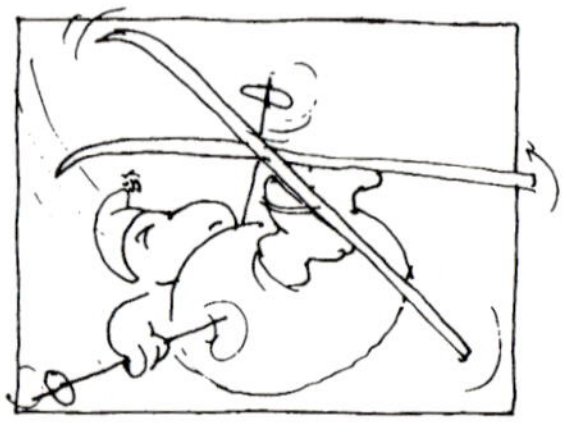

7 ____________________

8 ____________________

9 ____________________

10 ____________________

11 ____________________

12 ____________________

play football – ride a bike – go fishing – skate – go skiing – swim – sail – dance – play tennis – collect stamps – climb a tree – ride a horse

Ü 10.3. Over to you

Now write down what you can do and what you can't.

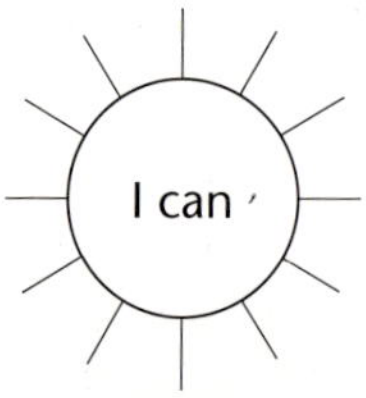

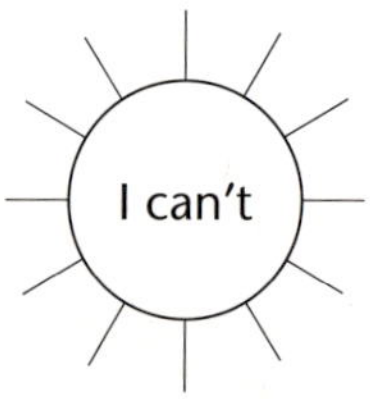

Ü 10.4. Classroom talk

What do you or your teacher say in class when …
Look at the phrases below.

du etwas nicht verstehst — I can't understand that.

du Hilfe brauchst

du etwas nicht gut sehen kannst

dein Lehrer etwas wiederholen soll

du etwas nicht tun kannst, weil es zu schwierig ist

du wissen willst, wie etwas geschrieben wird

du das Fenster öffnen möchtest

dein Lehrer deine Hausaufgaben sehen will

du an die Tafel schreiben willst

du etwas ausgesprochen haben willst

I can't do it, it's too difficult. – Can you say that again, please? – Can you help me? – I can't see very well. – I can't understand that. – Can you show me your homework? – Can I open the window? – Can you pronounce this word? – Can I write that word on the board? – Can you spell that word, please?

Ü 10.5. Fred's broken arm

Fred broke his arm two weeks ago. When he came out of hospital there were many things he couldn't do without help.
Which of these things do you think he could do and which things couldn't he do.

go out for a walk – play the guitar – climb trees – wash his hair – go to school – open bottles – go to bed – do his homework – take a shower –use his computer – eat with a spoon –

Example: Fred couldn't climb trees with his broken arm.

Could

Could wird auch als Hilfsverb zum Ausdrücken einer höflichen Bitte gebraucht.
Merke dir, dass man im Englischen im Allgemeinen höflicher miteinander redet als bei uns.

Ü 10.6. Could you please?

Complete the dialogues.

+	Yes, you can. Yes, of course.	–	No, you can't.

use

A) I'm late! Could I use your bike? +

B) Yes, of course.

take

A) It's raining. Could I ___________

your _______________? +

B) Yes, you can.

meet

A) Mary is at the station.

_______________________ her?

B) No, _________________

[–]

meet – treffen, abholen

use

A) I'm tired. _______________________

your ________?

B) _______________________

[+]

use

A) I want to play tennis.

_______________________ racket?

B) _______________________

[–]

must / mustn't / needn't

Die Grundbedeutung von *must* ist „müssen". Fragen werden mit *must?* gebildet. Die Verneinung von *must* ist *needn't*.

Mustn't heißt „nicht dürfen".

Must, mustn't und *needn't* werden nur in der Gegenwartsform (Präsens) benutzt.

Ü 10.7. Filling in

Complete the following sentences.

1. Fred's arm is broken, he __must__ go to the hospital.
2. He can walk to the hospital, he __needn't__ call the ambulance.
3. He _________________ stay in the building and he _________________ stay in bed.
4. Because he is ill, he ____________________ go to school.
5. As a good patient he ____________________ do what the doctors tell him. He ____________________ take the medicine, he ____________________ tell what he has got, but he ____________________ tell everything.
6. Fred is very happy that he ____________________ stay for a long time and can go home after one week.

Ü 10.8. Mother is ill in bed

You must help with the housework. Your friends want to play with you.

Your friends:		**You:**
Come on, let's go ... to the beach	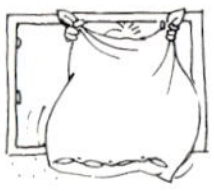	Sorry, I can't. I must make the beds.
sailing	______________________	
to the zoo		______________________
to the football match	______________________	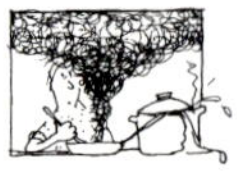
swimming		______________________
to the park	______________________	
out		______________________

Ü 10.9. Traffic signs

Look at the traffic signs and complete the sentences.

Here you find a number of situations in which the driver must drive carefully.

The car ___mustn't turn___ (not / turn) left.

It ___must turn___ (turn) right.

The car driver ______________________ (watch) out for the zebra crossing.

He ______________________. (slow down)

slow down – hier: langsamer fahren

The cyclist ______________________ (not / enter) the road.

He ______________________ (drive) in the other direction.

The car driver ____________________ (not / open) the door.

He ____________________ (look) in the mirror first.

The car driver ____________________ (wait) because the other ____________________ has the right of way.

Ü 10.10. A street scene

Look at the picture. Colour in the picture and answer the questions.

1. How many and what kind of vehicles can you see?
2. How many people can you see?
3. What kind of shops are there?
4. Write down, what the people must do or mustn't do. Think of the driver of the motorbike / of the lorry, the people on the zebra crossing etc.

vehicle – Fahrzeug

Example: The driver of the motorbike must slow down because there are people on the zebra crossing.

Übungsziel:
Die Satzstellung bei Fragesätzen mit und ohne Hilfsverb / to be kennen lernen

11. Questions and Negations

statements	questions
Fred must lie in bed.	*Must Fred lie in bed?*
Mary must do that again.	*Must Mary do that again?*
My father can play the piano.	*Can my father play the piano?*
The teacher could do it well.	*Could the teacher do it well?*
We will be back at 3 o'clock.	*Will we be back at 3 o'clock?*
Fred has got a dog.	*Has Fred got a dog?*
They are doing their homework.	*Are they doing their homework?*
Ricky goes shopping.	*Does Ricky go shopping?*
They play tennis.	*Do they play tennis?*

Wenn im Aussagesatz ein Hilfsverb oder eine Form des Verbs *to be* vorhanden ist, rückt das Hilfsverb bzw. diese Form an den Anfang des Satzes vor das Subjekt – wie im Deutschen.

Wenn weder ein Hilfsverb noch eine Form von *to be* vorhanden ist, musst du eine Frage mit dem Hilfsverb *to do* einleiten.

Anders als im Deutschen darfst du im Englischen eine Frage nie mit einem Vollverb beginnen.

	subject	**predicate**	**object**	
	Peter	*can understand*	*English*	**statement**
Can	*Peter*	*understand*	*English*	**question**

	subject	**predicate**	**object**	
	Peter	*plays*	*football*	**statement**
Does	*Peter*	*play*	*football*	**question**

Das -s in der 3. Person Singular wandert mit dem *do* an den Anfang des Satzes.

Bei der Umschreibung mit *do / does* steht das Vollverb immer im Infinitiv und hat nie die Endung *-s* in der 3. Person Singular.

Hier noch ein Überblick über die Formen von *to do*:

	present tense				Verneinung
Singular	I	do	my	exercises	don't do my exercises
	you	do	your	exercises	don't do your exercises
	he		his		his
	she	**does**	her	exercises	**doesn't do** her exercises
	it		its		its
Plural	we	do	our	exercises	don't do our exercises
	you	do	your	exercises	don't do your exercises
	they	do	their	exercises	don't do their exercises

	past tense				Verneinung
Singular	I	did	my	exercises	didn't do my exercises
	you	did	your	exercises	didn't do your exercises
	he		his		his
	she	**did**	her	exercises	**didn't do** her exercises
	it		its		its
Plural	we	did	our	exercises	didn't do our exercises
	you	did	your	exercises	didn't do your exercises
	they	did	their	exercises	didn't do their exercises

Die Vollform für die Verneinung heißt ***do not* / *does not*** und ***did not***.

Ü 11.1. Question form

Change the statements to question form.

1. He can swim very well. *Can he swim very well?*
2. They may sit here. ____________________?
3. I can understand everything. ____________________?
4. You mustn't smoke here. ____________________?
5. She will telephone us later. ____________________?

Ü 11.2. Scrambled questions

Write down the statements in the right order and change the sentences to question form.

1. My | is | garage | father | in | the

My father is in the garage.

Question: Is my father in the garage?

2. The | is | cat | walking | wall | the | on

____

Question: ______________________________?

3. Mother | windows | cleaning | the | is

____

Question: ______________________________?

4. The | are | in | playground | playing | children | the

____

Question: ______________________________?

5. The | are | round | running | the | lions | cage

____

Question: ______________________________?

6. The | getting | bus | boys | are | the | on

____

Question: ______________________________?

Ü 11.3. Mixed exercise

Write down the questions.

1. German / is / she ______________________? Yes, she is.
2. Peter Brown / are / you ______________________? No, I'm not.
3. Father / football / playing / is ______________________? No, he isn't.
4. the window / open / is ______________________? Yes, it is.
5. I / go / out / may ______________________? Yes, you may.
6. Sheila / write / a letter / must ______________________? No, she needn't.

Ü 11.4. Questions with *does*

Ask questions and answer them.

1. Peter likes sport. __Does__ he play football?

   __Yes, he does.__

2. Jacko is a monkey. ________ it eat bananas? ______________.
3. Mrs. Black is a pilot. ________ she fly planes? ______________.
4. Brenda is a pupil. ________ she go to work? ______________.
5. John helps his mother in the garden. ________ he sell things?

   ______________.

Ü 11.5. Mixed questions

Ask questions with do / does.

1. The cat likes fish. __Does the cat like fish?__
2. You speak English. ______________________
3. Peter rides his bike. ______________________
4. I know my headmaster. ______________________
5. You often go to the cinema. ______________________
6. Teachers mark tests. ______________________
7. The pilot flies planes. ______________________
8. We play tennis every summer. ______________________
9. Children like sweets. ______________________
10. She lives on the second floor. ______________________

Ü 11.6. Scrambled questions

Can you ask questions? Write the correct questions in your exercise book.

1	Are	this your bike?	Yes, it is.	A
2	Do	he got a dog?	Yes, he has.	B
3	Am	you German?	Yes, I am.	C
4	Does	you go to school every day?	No, I don't.	D
5	Hasn't	you hear it?	No, I can't.	E
6	Is	I your friend?	Yes, you are.	F
7	Has	it in the garden?	No, it isn't.	G
8	Can	he live in New York?	Yes, he does.	H
9	Have	she got a budgie?	Yes, she has.	I
10	Can't	you got a bike?	Yes, I have.	J
11	Doesn't	you swim?	Yes, I can.	K
12	Isn't	he go to school by bus?	No, he doesn't.	L

1	2	3	4	5	6	7	8	9	10	11	12

Negation

Enthält der Satz ein Hilfsverb oder eine Form von *to be*, so wird für die Verneinung das Wort *not* gebraucht.
Can + *not* wird in einem Wort geschrieben: *cannot*. Die Kurzform heißt *can't*.

Die Kurzform von *will* + *not* heißt *won't*.

My father cannot / can't speak English.
The sun is not / isn't shining.
I hope my teacher will not / won't come back soon.

Ü 11.7. Filling in

Fill in the correct forms of the auxiliaries.

subject	predicate		object	auxiliary
1. Grandmother	cannot	play	football.	– can
2. The girls	___________	bake	a cake.	+ must
3. Lions	___________	read	books.	– can
4. Billy	___________	play	with his friend.	– could
5. The children	___________	listening	to the radio.	– be
6. Cats	___________	make	ice cream.	– can
7. Mother	___________	having	a bath.	+ be

Negations with *do / does*

Ist im Aussagesatz weder ein Hilfsverb noch eine Form von *to be* vorhanden, so wird für die Verneinung das Hilfsverb *to do* verwendet.

positive Frageform

do – *I / you / we / you / they*

does – *he / she / it*

verneinte Frageform

don't – *I / you / we / you / they*

doesn't – *he / she / it*

	subject	predicate	object	
	He	*doesn't play*	*football*	**statement**
Doesn't	*he*	*play*	*football*	**question**

Das *-s* der 3. Person Singular wandert bei der Verneinung vom Vollverb an die Form des Hilfsverbs *to do*.

Susan likes English lessons very much.

Susan doesn't like French lessons.

Das Verb hinter der Form von *to do* hat keine Endung. Es steht immer im Infinitiv.

Ü 11.8. Likes and dislikes – eating and drinking

Write down the answers in your exercise book.

Example: I like juice but I don't like milk.

biscuits

juice

potatoes

toast

tomatoes

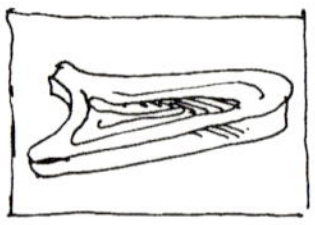
meat

onions

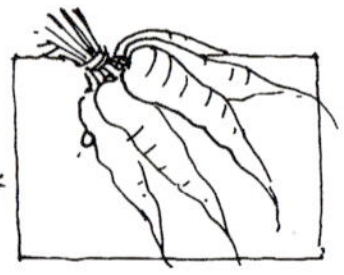
carrots

chocolate

rice

cake

milk

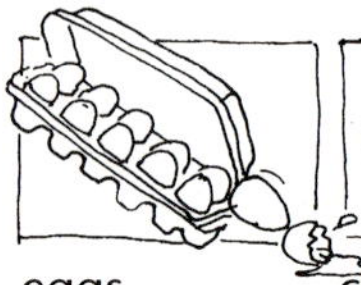
eggs

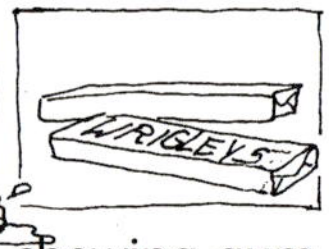

chewing-gum

coffee

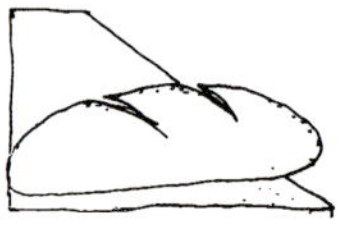
bread

water

jam

lemonade

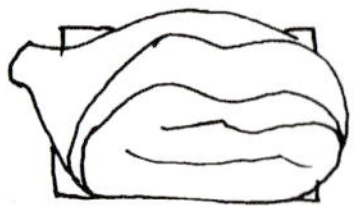
bacon

Ü 11.9. Over to you

What do you do and what don't you do? Write down the answers in your exercise book.

Do you live with your parents?	Do you play tennis?	Do you often go swimming in summer?	Do you know how to dance?
Do you often watch television?	Do your friends often play games with you?	Do you like school?	Do you walk to school every day?
Do you like watching football games?	Do you go to school by bus?	Do you like maths?	Do you do your homework in the afternoon?
Do you do your homework in the evening?	Do you like pets?	Do you collect stamps?	Do you some-times go to a pop concert?
Do you sometimes go to a disco?	Do your friends often go to a disco?	Do you like going shopping?	Do you buy sweets with your pocket money?
Do you get money if you help your parents?	Do you get enough pocket money?	Do you some-times get money as a present?	Do you buy clothes with your pocket money?
Do you have any brothers and sisters?	Do you live in a house?	Do you live in town?	

Ü 11.10. The likes and dislikes of Mr. Brown

Complete the sentences. Use the phrases below.

work – doing the washing-up – going to work – driving the car – listening to music – going out – cleaning the car – drinking beer – reading the newspaper – drinking tea

+

Mr. Brown likes drinking beer but he doesn't like drinking tea.

−

+

Mr. Brown likes ...

−

+

−

+

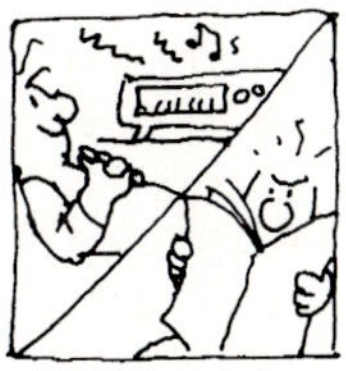

−

+

−

*Übungsziel:
Den Gebrauch von Fragewörtern kennen lernen*

12. Question Words

Mit den Fragewörtern *what* und *who(m)* fragt man nach Sachen, Handlungen oder Personen im Objektfall. Mit *where* und *when* fragt man nach Ort und Zeit als adverbiale Bestimmung.

What? ⟶ fragt nach Handlungen oder Sachen (Objekt) – was?
things

I see a house.

What do you see?

Who(m)? ⟶ fragt nach Personen (Objekt) – wen / wem?
persons

We help our mother in the house.

Who(m) do we help?

Where? ⟶ fragt nach dem Ort (adverbiale Bestimmung) – wo / woher / wohin?
place

I am from London.

Where are you from?

When? ⟶ fragt nach der Zeit (adverbiale Bestimmung) – wann?
time

Next year I am going to London.

When do you go to London?

Wie die Fragestellung funktioniert, weißt du schon aus dem letzten Kapitel: Befindet sich ein Hilfsverb oder eine Form von *to be* im Satz, dann wird die Frage damit gebildet.

I can speak English. *What can you speak?*

Befindet sich kein Hilfsverb oder eine Form von *to be* im Satz, dann wird die Frage mit einer Form von *to do* umschrieben. Es folgt dann das Vollverb im Infinitiv.

We like apples. *What do we like?*

Auch hier wandert dann das *-s* in der 3. Person Singular an die Form von *to do*.

Mrs. Black drinks wine. *What does Mrs. Black drink?*

Ü 12.1. Questions with *what*

Ask questions with what *to get these answers:*

1. A.: Father likes beer.

   Q.: What does father like?

2. A.: David is doing his homework.

   Q.: ______________________________?

3. A.: The bikes need new tyres.

   Q.: ______________________________?

tyre – Reifen

4. A.: The children are playing ball.

   Q.: ______________________________?

Ü 12.2. *What* and *who(m)*

Ask questions about the underlined words.

1. Pamela wants a new dress. What does Pamela want?
2. Mother feeds the little baby. Who does mother feed?
3. Peter buys apples in the shop. ______________________________?
4. Bob and Pat love their parents. ______________________________?
5. My son meets his girlfriend in town.

   ______________________________?
6. We like to watch the football players.

   ______________________________?
7. The girls learn a new song. ______________________________?
8. They love your apple cake. ______________________________?
9. Father buys a little toy for his daughter.

   ______________________________?
10. Mrs. Brown likes a cup of coffee after lunch.

    ______________________________?

Ü 12.3. *Where?*

Ask questions and answer them. Write them down in your exercise book.

Example: Where are you staying? I am staying at home.

stay – sich aufhalten

Where are you going? **Where are you staying?**

to school

to the sportsground

in church

at home

to the park

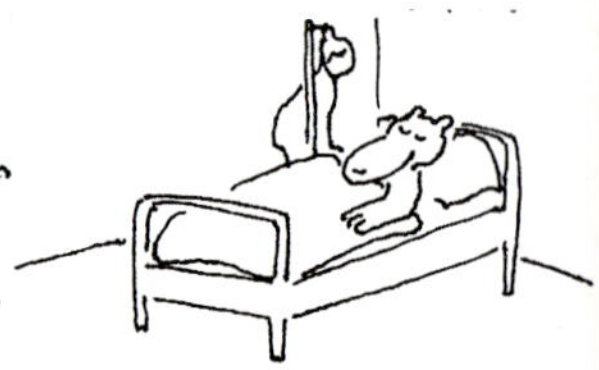

in hospital

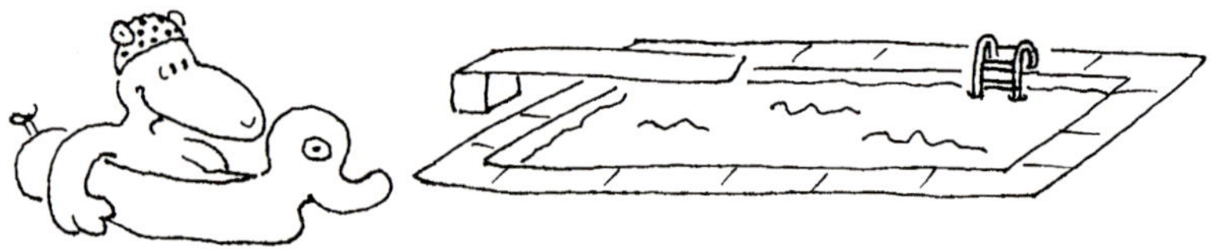

to the pool

Ü 12.4. Asking questions

Ask questions about the underlined words.

1. The boys play football in the sportsground. Where do the boys play?
2. Bob watches television at home. ____________________?
3. Mrs. Brown stays at home every Wednesday. ____________________?
4. The children go to church to sing songs. ____________________?
5. Pam and Peter go to the park for a walk. ____________________?
6. We swim in the pool every weekend. ____________________?

Ü 12.5. *When?*

Form questions to get the answers below.

Questions		**Answers**
1. begin / school	When does school begin?	At eight o'clock.
2. we / have / tea	________________________________?	In the afternoon.
3. our parents / we / help	________________________________?	After school.
4. the alarm-clock / ring	________________________________?	At 6.30 in the morning.
5. they / their teeth / brush	________________________________?	Every morning and evening.

Ü 12.6. What do you do on weekdays?

Answer the questions.

When do you get up?

____

When do you have breakfast?

____

What time do you go to school?

____

When do you do your homework?

____

When do you have supper?

____

What time do you go to bed?

____

More question words

Which? selection	→ fragt nach der Auswahl von Personen und Sachen aus einer bestimmten Anzahl *Which do you like better, coffee or milk?* *Which of you was first?*	– welche(r)?
Whose? possession	→ fragt nach dem Besitz *Whose hat is this?*	– wessen?
Why? reason	→ fragt nach dem Grund als Antwort: *because …* *Why do you get up so late?* *Because I feel ill today.*	– warum?
How? manner	→ fragt nach der Art und Weise *How are you? Fine, thanks.*	– wie?
How much? quantity	→ fragt nach der Menge (uncountables) *How much sugar have we got?*	– wie viel?
How many? number	→ fragt nach der Anzahl (countables) *How many shirts have you got?*	– wie viele?
How often? number (time)	→ fragt nach der Häufigkeit *How often do you go to school?*	– wie oft?

Ü 12.7. An interview

Finish this interview by filling in the question words.

1. ______________	do you get up in the morning?	At 6.15.
2. ______________	do you have breakfast?	In the kitchen.
3. ______________	do you come to school?	I ride my bike.
4. ______________	does your teacher come to school?	By car.
5. ______________	do you come home?	At 1.45.
6. ______________	do you want for dinner?	Spaghetti.

7. ______________ do you do in the afternoon? I meet my friends.

8. ______________ do you meet your friends? In the park.

9. ______________ do you watch TV? In the evening.

Ü 12.8. *How often?*

Ask and answer questions. Write them down in your exercise book.

Example: How often do you travel by train? – Quite often.

always – every day – every week – every month – quite often – sometimes – about once (twice) a week (month) – not very often – hardly ever – never

get up early

eat alone

go to school by bike

see your neighbour driving his car

have lessons in the afternoon

eat spaghetti

meet your best friend

meet your friends in the park

watch TV

Ü 12.9. Why must I do that?

Mother and son are talking. Fill in why and because.

Son: Mummy, ______________ have I got to learn English?

Mother: ______________ it's good for you.

Son: But ______________ have I got to learn it when I don't like it?

Mother: ______________ you'll need it.

Son: But, Mummy, ______________ have I got to learn English when it's so hard?

Mother: ______________ you have to!

Ü 12.10. The wheel of questions

Write the questions in the right order in your exercise book.

Who? – what?

Fragst du nach dem Subjekt eines Satzes, so wird die Frage mit *who* oder *what* eingeleitet:

> *who* fragt nach Personen;
> *what* fragt nach Sachen.

Wenn wir mit *who* oder *what* nach dem Subjekt des Satzes fragen, gibt es keine Umschreibung mit *to do*:

	subject	**predicate**	**object**
statement	*Fred*	*likes*	*bananas.*
question	*Who*	*likes*	*bananas?*

	subject	**predicate**	**object**
statement	*The bikes*	*belong*	*to Brenda.*
question	*What*	*belongs*	*to Brenda?*

Nach *who* und *what* hat das Vollverb im Fragesatz immer ein *-s*. Es ist dabei egal, ob das Subjekt des entsprechenden Aussagesatzes im Singular oder im Plural steht:

> *Who likes bananas? – Fred.*
> *Who likes bananas? – The children.*

Die Form des Hilfsverbs bleibt, wie sie ist:

> *Who can come to the party?*

Ü 12.11. *Who?*

Ask questions with who that get these answers:

1. Q.: Who is with Brenda? A.: It's her boyfriend Paul. 

2. Q.: ______________________? A.: Father washes the car. 

3. Q.: ______________________? A.: Molly has a dog. 

4. Q.: ______________________? A.: Peter and Paul like fish. 

5. Q.: ______________________? A.: John is Brenda's brother. 

6. Q.: ______________________ can speak English? A.: We all can. 

Ü 12.12. Who is doing what?

Write the answers down in your exercise book.

1. Who is reading a book?
2. Who is writing a letter?
3. Who is painting a picture?
4. Who is watching TV?
5. Who is listening to the radio?
6. Who is singing?
7. Who is swimming?
8. Who is sleeping?
9. Who is eating an apple?
10. Who is drinking tea?
11. Who is playing football?
12. Who is playing tennis?

Who and *where*

Who und *where* werden leicht verwechselt. Dieses Schema kann dir eine Merkhilfe sein:

there ◄—— *where?*   *who?* ——► *you*

where? ↓ wo?   *who?* ↓ wer?

Ü 12.13. *Who?* oder *where?*

Form questions to get these answers.

1. ______________	is Brenda's sister?	Her sister is Mary.
2. ______________	is father now?	He's in the garden.
3. ______________	is that boy over there?	That's Peter.
4. ______________	is my English book?	It's on your desk.
5. ______________	are you going this afternoon?	I am going to the beach.
6. ______________	is that over there?	It's our English teacher.
7. ______________	is your coat?	It's in the wardrobe.
8. ______________	is playing football?	Peter and Henry.

Ü 12.14. Mixed questions

Write questions to the following answers. Your questions must be based on the underlined words.

Frag nach den unterstrichenen Wörtern.

1. They are going to school this morning. *Where are they going?*
2. The film begins at 6 pm. ______________________?
3. Pat buys two new shirts. ______________________?
4. We have seen the film three times. ______________________?
5. Richard lives in London. ______________________?
6. Susan is very sad because she is ill. ______________________?
7. John's wife is called Mary. ______________________?
8. They have gone to France for two weeks. ______________________?
9. We are staying at our cousin's. ______________________?
10. The bike costs £120. ______________________?
11. Peter goes to school by bus. ______________________?
12. Tom is an assistant in a shop. ______________________?
13. The shop sells newspapers, pens and pencils.

    ____?
14. The last exercise is very hard. ______________________?
15. There are more than 5000 people at the concert.

    ____?

16. Thomas is happy because he got a good school report.

____?

17. Peter and Henry are playing football. ______________________?

18. Aunt Mary's coat is in the bedroom. ______________________?

19. Janet doesn't like spaghetti. ______________________?

20. We had to wait over half an hour. ______________________?

21. Fred weighs 70 kilos. ______________________?

22. My English book is on the desk. ______________________?

Ü 12.15. Interviewing people

A famous pop star is in your town. You and other reporters ask her / him a lot of questions. Write them down in your exercise book and answer them.

Questions	Answers
Where do you …?	I live in … My home is near …
What do you like?	I like … I'm fond of …
What do you hate?	I don't like …
Do you like …? How do you like …? What is your favourite …? What kind of … do you like? Which music …?	My favourite … is

Questions	Answers
What are your plans for …? What will you do …? Where will you …? When will you …?	I will … I'm going to …
Have you ever been to … before?	Yes, I have … No, I've never …
Do you speak …? Do you understand …?	No, I don't speak …
What did you do …? When did you …? Where did you …?	
Have you got a lot of …?	Yes, I've got a lot of fans in …

Übungsziel:
Am Bahnhof Auskünfte einholen und Fahrkarten kaufen können

13. At the Station

Ü 13.1. Illustrated vocabulary

Match the numbers to the words. Colour in and describe the picture. Write down what you can see.

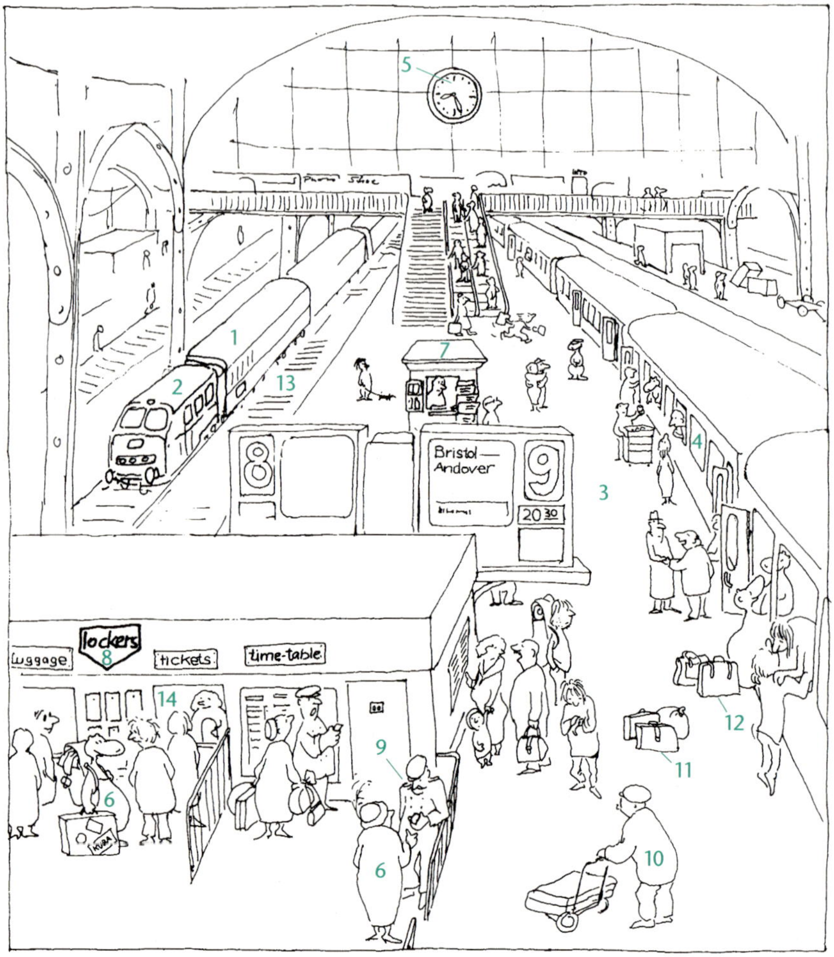

station

- ☐ train / engine
- ☐ platform
- ☐ passengers
- ☐ newsstand
- ☐ guard
- ☐ luggage
- ☐ rails
- ☐ ticket office
- ☐ suitcase
- ☐ porter
- ☐ locker
- ☐ station-clock
- ☐ compartment

Ü 13.2. At the railway station

Fill in the words from the list.

People buy ____________ for the ____________. They get ____________ and ____________ the trains. ____________ carry suitcases.

suitcase – Koffer

____________ wait for the trains on a ____________. At the ____________ people buy ____________.

Some people are ____________. They hurry to get the train.

platform – ticket office – trains – on – off – passengers – porters – late – tickets

Asking a railway official

Redeabsicht	Redemittel
einen Bahnangestellten ansprechen	*Can you help me, please?*
nach der Abfahrts- oder Ankunftszeit fragen	*When does the train to … leave?* *When does the next train from … arrive?*
nach dem Bahnsteig fragen	*Which platform does the train to … leave from?* *Which platform does the train from … arrive at?*

At the ticket office

Redeabsicht	Redemittel
eine Hin- oder Rückfahrkarte kaufen	*A single ticket to …, please.* *A return ticket to …, please.*
eine Kinderfahrkarte kaufen	*A half single ticket to …, please.* *A half return ticket to …, please.*
nach dem Preis einer Fahrkarte fragen	*How much does it cost?* *How much is it?* *How much is a ticket to …?* *What does a ticket to … cost?*

Ü 13.3. Travelling by train

Read the dialogues.

Brenda: Can you help me, please?
Official: Yes?
Brenda: When does the next train to Birmingham leave?
Official: Wait a minute. The next train to Birmingham leaves at 14.02 (fourteen – oh – two).
Brenda: And when does it arrive?
Official: At 16.15.
Brenda: O. K. And which platform does it leave from?
Official: Platform 2.
Brenda: Thank you.
Official: You're welcome.

Lady: One and a half singles to Brighton, please.
Official: Is the half for that young gentleman?
Lady: Yes, he's my son.
Official: How old is he?
Lady: He's eleven.
Official: Is he? He looks a big boy for his age.
Lady: Yes, he does.
Official: One and a half to Brighton. That's £22, please.
Lady: Thanks. Come on, Fred. We're late.

return – Rückfahrkarte

Gentleman: Two tickets to London, please.
Official: Single or return?
Gentleman: How much is the single fare?
Official: £6.
Gentleman: Is the return cheaper than two singles?
Official: Yes, sir.
Gentleman: Two returns, then.
Official: Right! Two returns to London. £18, please.

Ü 13.4. A little rhyme

Learn it by heart.

There was a young lady named Sue
who wanted to catch the 2.02.
Said the porter, "Don't harry,
don't hurry or worry:
It's a minute or two to 2.02."

14. Food and Drink

Übungsziel: Nahrungsmittel und Getränke benennen können

Ü 14.1. Illustrated vocabulary

Write all the numbers of the things in the boxes.

1 eggs – 2 milk – 3 ice-cream – 4 spinach – 5 lemonade – 6 sandwiches – 7 fish – 8 bread – 9 cabbage – 10 rolls – 11 cheese – 12 oil – 13 mushrooms – 14 beans – 15 cucumber – 16 salt – 17 tomatoes – 18 potatoes – 19 cornflakes – 20 tea – 21 butter – 22 cake – 23 coffee – 24 ham – 25 vinegar

Write down in your exercise book what you like and what you don't like.

I think … is / are delicious.
I like …
I don't like …
I think … is / are horrible.

Ü 14.2. Colourful fruits and vegetables

Colour in the fruits and vegetables. You must look at the numbers. Write the names of the fruits and vegetables in the boxes.

1 light brown – 2 blue – 3 brown – 4 yellow – 5 orange – 6 dark green – 7 red – 8 green – 9 light green

The oranges are orange. The pears are yellow. The bananas are yellow. The plums are blue. The walnuts are brown. The mushrooms are light brown. The potatoes are brown. The apples are red and yellow. The cherries are red. The carrots are orange. The grapes are blue and green. The strawberries are red. The tomatoes are red. The pineapple is yellow, green and light green. The peas are green. The melon is dark green.

Ü 14.3. Wordsearch

Tipp: Such in alle Richtungen!

How many fruits and vegetables can you find in this box?

T	M	S	T	O	R	R	A	C	E	A	O
S	E	A	N	S	E	L	P	P	A	S	R
R	L	B	A	N	A	N	A	S	D	E	A
A	O	C	S	E	O	T	A	T	O	P	N
E	N	A	H	C	A	N	I	P	S	A	G
P	P	I	N	E	A	P	P	L	E	R	E
K	S	E	I	R	R	E	H	C	E	G	S
S	T	R	A	W	B	E	R	R	I	E	S
S	E	O	T	A	M	O	T	P	E	A	S

pineapple

Ü 14.4. What is it?

Fill in the gaps.

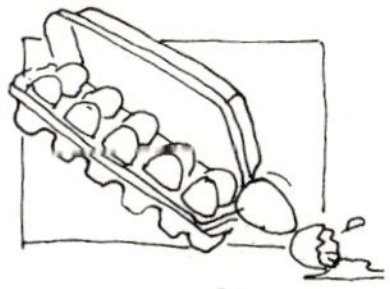

1. Hens lay them. They are ________________.

2. It's sweet, yellow, red or brown and sounds like pair. It's a ________________.

3. It's white and comes from cows. Children drink it often. It's ________________.

4. They're small and oval shaped, red or green. They're nice to eat and you sometimes make wine from them. They're ________________.

5. It's long, green and quite hard. You eat it in salads and sandwiches. It's a ________________.

6. When your hear or read its name, you think maybe it's a kind of apple. But it isn't. It's a ________________.

7. It's brown or green and made of leaves and hot water. You drink it. It's ________________.

8. It's light or dark yellow. It's made of milk. You eat it with bread. It's ________________.

9. You may think they're a kind of room. You'll never be able to go inside one, but you can eat them. They're ________________.

Countables and uncountables

zählbare und nicht zählbare Hauptwörter

nouns

countables	***uncountables***
können gezählt werden, können im Singular und im Plural gebraucht werden	können nicht gezählt werden, können nicht im Plural gebraucht werden
books, windows, tables, apples	*butter, jam, sugar, milk*

Ü 14.5. Make a list

Write down which words are countables and which are uncountables.

coffee, apple, cornflakes, car, rice, sugar

countables	uncountables

milk, saucer, butter, chair, desk, orange juice

Much and many

Much und *many* bedeuten viel / viele.

Much kann nur vor *uncountable nouns* stehen.

Many steht nur vor *countable nouns*.

Examples:

much water	viel Wasser	***but***	*many cars*	viele Autos
much money	viel Geld	***but***	*many houses*	viele Häuser
much milk	viel Milch	***but***	*many apples*	viele Äpfel

Ü 14.6. Planning a party

You are planning a party and you must decide with your friend how much / how many you need. Write the answers in your exercise book.

coke

How much cola do we need?

crackers

tomatoes

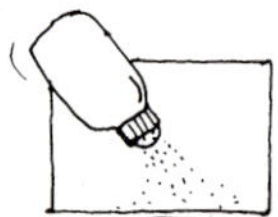

salt

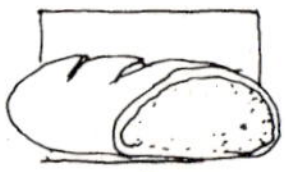

bread

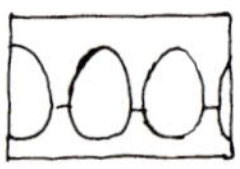

eggs

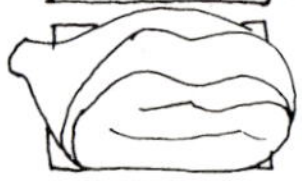

bacon

lemonade

sugar

milk

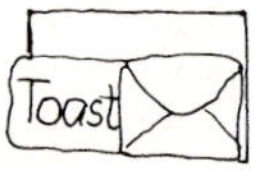

toast

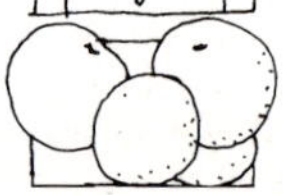

oranges

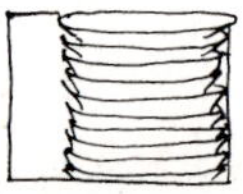

plates

Ü 14.7. The food game

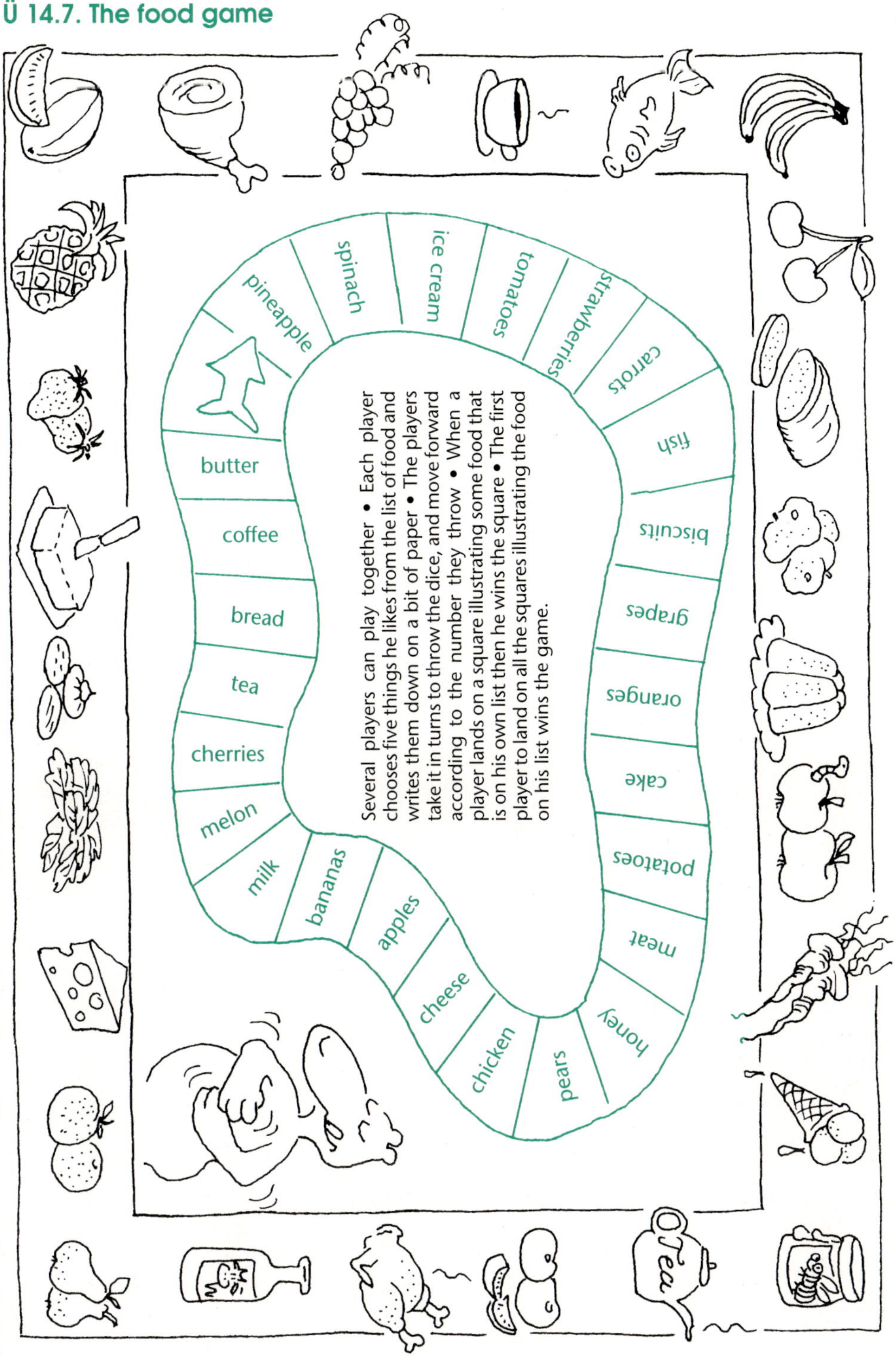

An diesem Spiel können zwei oder mehrere Kinder teilnehmen • Jeder Spieler schreibt auf ein Blatt Papier fünf oder mehr Sachen zum Essen, die hier präsentiert werden • Abwechselnd würfeln und vom Pfeil ausgehend um die gewürfelte Zahl vorrücken • Man bekommt die Speise, bei der der Spielstein stehen geblieben ist, jedoch nur, wenn sie auf der eigenen Liste steht • Gewinner ist, wer nach einer oder mehreren Runden als Erster alle Speisen seiner Liste bekommen hat.

Ü 14.8. The three magic apples

basket – Korb

Andy was on the number nine bus on his way home from school. At Park Road an old woman got onto the bus. She had a big basket of apples. Andy saw her and stood up. "Would you like a seat?" he said. "Thank you very much," the woman said and she gave Andy three big red apples. When she gave him the apples, Andy heard the words:

Tell the apple
what you want to be.
Eat it and see what you will see.

park bench – Parkbank

Andy thanked her and put the apples into his school bag. It was like a dream. When he got home, he had lunch and then he did his homework. Then he took the apples, ran out into the park and sat down on a park bench. He saw some tall boys playing football.

"I want to be tall and strong," Andy said and began to eat the first apple. Suddenly he was very tall and strong. Now he wanted to play with the big boys, so he went over to them, took the ball and kicked it high into the air. When the boys saw that he was so strong, they ran away. Andy was sad because he wanted to have a lot of friends.

"I want to be famous," he said and began to eat the second apple. "When I am famous, I will have a lot of friends." Suddenly there were hundreds of people around him. They had cameras and microphones and they wanted interviews with him. He did not know what to say, so he ran away. The reporters followed him. When he came to a road, he saw a fine sports car.

"I want to be rich. Then I could have this beautiful car," Andy said and quickly began to eat his third apple. Suddenly he was rich. He had a sports car, he had a helicopter, and he lived in a very big and beautiful house. He had everything, but he was not happy.

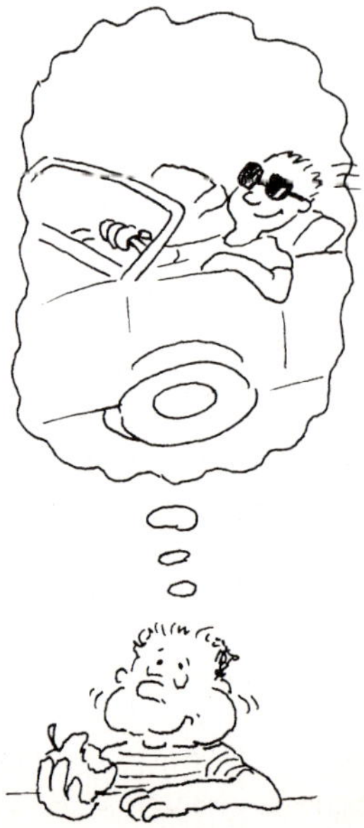

One night he had a dream. In his dream he saw the old woman again. "I am unhappy," he said, "I do not want to be tall and strong, famous and rich." The old woman looked at him. "Go into the garden and find a small yellow flower," she said. At that moment Andy heard the words:

Tell the flower
What you want to be
Smell it and see what you will see.

Andy ran into the garden. He found the flower near the apple tree. "I want to be me," he said and suddenly he was on the park bench again. "Come and play with us," the boys said to him. Andy stood up and ran over.

True or false? Tick.

	true	false
1. Andy wanted to go shopping.		
2. The woman gave Andy some fruit.		
3. Andy ate the apples before lunch.		
4. When Andy began to eat the first apple he changed into a strong and tall boy.		
5. The other boys were afraid of him.		
6. Andy liked talking to the reporters.		
7. When Andy saw the sports car, he took it.		
8. Andy was strong, rich and very happy.		
9. Andy saw the old woman in his dream.		
10. Andy wanted to be a flower.		
11. The boys wanted to play with Andy.		

Find the facts. Write them down in your exercise book.

Where did Andy meet an old woman?
What did she give Andy?
What did Andy do when he got home?
Andy ate three apples. What did he want to be?
Andy kicked the ball into the air. What did the boys do?
What did Andy do when the reporters asked a lot of questions?
Andy was rich. What did he have?
Who did he see in his dreams?
What did Andy find in the garden?

Meal times

Übungsziel: Die britischen Mahlzeiten kennen lernen

The British usually have four meals a day.

During the week breakfast is usually cereal, some toast and coffee. But on Sunday it's something special: bacon and eggs and then toast and marmalade.

The meal in the middle of the day is lunch with soup, meat or chicken, peas, carrots and potatoes.

Tea time is the third meal of the day. It's everybody's favourite, especially for people who like sweet food: delicious cake with jam and cream and a cup of tea, of course.

The last meal of the day is dinner or supper . Supper is like dinner but it is not so large.

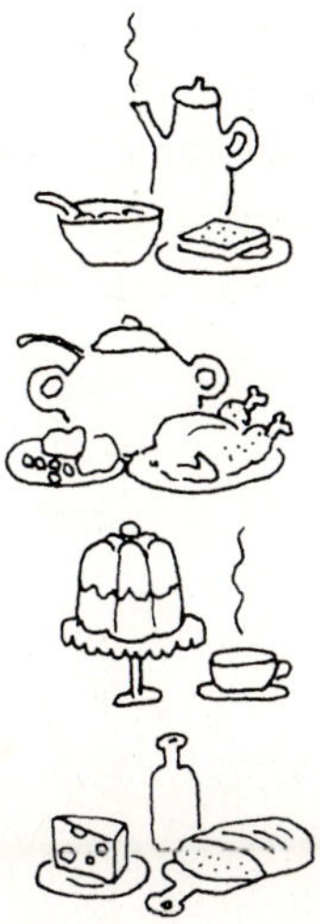

Ü 14.9. Meal time

Fill in the gaps.

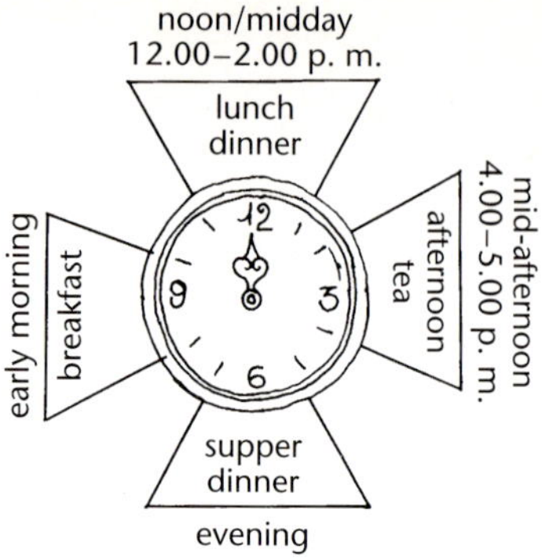

a. m. 1. It's ______________ in the morning.

The Evans are having ______________.

p. m. 2. It's ______________ in the evening.

The Evans are having ______________.

3. It's ______________. Now it's time for ______________.

p. m. 4. It's ______________ in the afternoon.

The family is having ______________.

Ü 14.10. Breakfast with Fred

Look at the picture. Describe what you see. Use the words at the side.

frying-pan – Bratpfanne

kettle – Kessel

mug – Becher

matchbox – Streichholzschachtel

tube – Tube

jar – Krug

tin – Dose

frying-pan
basket
kettle
cup
mug
saucepan
teapot
plate
bottle
matchbox
tube
jar
tin
bag

Ü 14.11. A letter home

Jenny, a British girl, is staying with a German family, the Schröters. This is her first letter home.

Dear Mum and Dad,

I like it very much here in Kiel and the Schröters are a very nice family. It's fine on the beach and we go sailing every day. But there are two or three things I miss very much here in Germany. Most people start work at 7.30 – and if I want to have breakfast with the Schröters I have to get up at half past six. Mr. Schröter is already in the kitchen at that time and makes the coffee. They almost all drink coffee in the morning. A little later Mrs. Schröter comes down the stairs and lays the table for breakfast.

We usually have toast and brown bread for breakfast. But the brown bread is not like our English brown bread. It's very dry and hard. We sometimes have a boiled egg, but mostly we eat cheese and meat on our bread.

Horrible! Cheese and meat in the morning! But sometimes we also have jam and honey.

The Schröters must like their breakfast. They have the same meal in the evening, too, only this time with juice or tea and no coffee.

Love

Jenny

Answer the following questions:

What does Jenny do every day?

___

When must Jenny get up in the morning?

___

Why does Mrs. Schröter go downstairs?

___

Which things does Mrs. Schröter put on the table? Name four things.

___

What do the English have for breakfast?

___

Ü 14.12. Over to you

What do you like for breakfast? Write the answers in your exercise book.

I like … I don't like … I hate … I'm fond of …

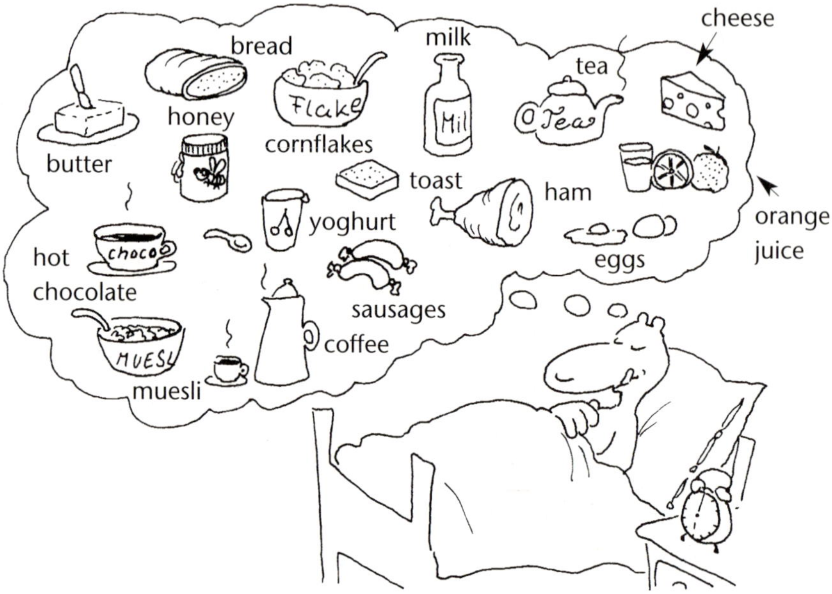

What do you like for lunch?

At the restaurant

Übungsziel:
Sich in einem Restaurant verständigen können

In a restaurant there are many people, the customers, the waiters and waitresses.

The waiters and waitresses ask the customers what they want. The customers look at the menu and say what they want. Then the waiters and waitresses serve their customers. Afterwards the customer asks for the bill and pays it. Most times he gives the waiter a tip.

bill – Rechnung

tip – Trinkgeld

What you can say at the table

Can I have | the … / some … / some more … / a / an … / a / an … of … / another … of … | please?

Can you | pass the … / hand me a … | please?

Hand me / Pass | the … / a … | please.

— Here you are

Can I bring you | a … / another … / a … of … / some … / some more …

Some more …?
Do you like …?
Would you like …?

— Thank you / Thanks / No, thank you / Yes, please

Ü 14.13. Dialogues

Make up dialogues. Write them down in your exercise book.

Examples:

Der Kellner fragt, ob du noch ein Glas Mineralwasser möchtest.
Du bedankst dich und lehnst ab.
Waiter: Can I bring you another glass of water?
You: No, thank you.

Du fragst, ob der Kellner dir das Salz geben kann.
Er bejaht und gibt dir das Salz.
You: Can you pass the salt, please?
Waiter: Here you are.

Der Kellner fragt dich, ob du noch ein Stück Brot haben willst.
Du bejahst.

Du fragst, ob du noch etwas Erbsen haben kannst.
Der Kellner bejaht und gibt dir welche.

Die Kellnerin fragt, ob du noch eine Tasse Kaffee haben möchtest.
Du bedankst dich, lehnst aber ab.

Der Kellner fragt, ob du noch von dem Hühnchen haben willst.
Du verneinst.

Du fragst, ob die Kellnerin dir noch etwas Kartoffeln geben kann. Außerdem hättest du gerne noch Pfeffer.
Die Kellnerin gibt dir den Pfeffer, bedauert aber, dass die Kartoffeln ausgegangen sind.

A menu

Evan's Restaurant

23 Piccadilly London

Menu

Starters

Tomato salad	£ 2.65
Grapefruit	£ 2.00
Soup of the day	£ 1.80

Main Course

Chicken and chips	£ 4.80
Steak and beans and potatoes	£ 7.50
Fried eggs and chips	£ 3.40
Roast pork with boiled potatoes	£ 5.50
Rosemary lamb	£ 5.80
Chicken legs	£ 4.85

Desserts

Apple pie and fresh cream	£ 2.80
Ice-cream – vanilla	£ 2.20
or chocolate topped	£ 2.40
Baked apples	£ 2.60
Fruit salad	£ 2.50

Drinks

Large mug of coffee	£ 2.80
Pot of tea per person	£ 1.80
Iced soft drinks:	
Cola	£ 2.50
Orange lemonade	£ 2.80
Harplayer beer ½ pint	£ 2.70
White wine by the glass	£ 2.80

No service charge included

Ü 14.14. Your own restaurant

Make a menu for your own restaurant. Write down as many things as you can. Think of starters, main courses, desserts and drinks.

What you can say in a restaurant

You:

Waiter,	can	I	have	the	menu	please?
Waitress,		we			pepper	
Excuse me,						
Miss,	can	you	bring	me		
				us		

Waiter:

Yes, of course. Here you are.
One moment, please.

What would you like	to eat?
	to drink?

You:

I would like …
I'd prefer …

Waiter:
That will take a little time.
In about half an hour.
Sorry, the … are off.

Are you satisfied?	
Are you happy with	the meal?
	the drinks?

You:

The	meal	was	too cold.
	steak		too hot.
	chicken		excellent.
	chips	were	very good.
			nice.
			not bad.
			not very warm.
			not very nice.

Can	I	have the bill, please?
	we	

Waiter:
Yes, of course. Here you are.
One moment, please.

Ü 14.15. A dialogue

Write the following dialogue in your exercise book.

Waiter	***You***
begrüßt dich	*Good afternoon.*
______________	möchtest die Karte haben
legt sie dir auf den Tisch	______________
______________	möchtest bestellen

fragt, was du essen willst → ______________________

______________________ ← sagst, was du haben möchtest

bedauert, dass ein Gericht nicht da ist → ______________________

______________________ ← suchst etwas anderes aus

fragt, ob du etwas trinken möchtest → ______________________

______________________ ← bestellst etwas zu trinken

fragt, ob du zufrieden bist → ______________________

______________________ ← sagst, dass das Essen gut war

bedankt sich und fragt, ob du noch Kaffee möchtest → ______________________

______________________ ← lehnst ab und fragst nach der Rechnung

nennt den Preis → ______________________

______________________ ← bezahlst und gibst Trinkgeld

bedankt sich, wünscht einen schönen Tag → ______________________

Übungsziel:
Die britische Währung kennen lernen.

15. Money, Money, Money

Die britische Währungseinheit ist das Pfund *(pound)*. Abgekürzt schreibt man dafür £. Ein *pound* hat 100 *pence*. Die Einzahl von *pence* heißt *penny*. Die Abkürzung von *penny* und *pence* ist p [piː]. Wenn man Preise schreibt, dann setzt man die Abkürzung £ vor den Preis wie DM im Deutschen. Aber wenn man spricht, sagt man erst den Preis und dann *pound* – ebenfalls wie im Deutschen.

£1	→ one pound / a pound
£1.25	→ one (pound) twenty-five
£2	→ two pounds
£11.60	→ eleven (pounds) sixty

1 p	→ one penny
8 p	→ eight pence
97 p	→ ninety-seven pence

Die Abkürzung für *penny* und *pence* setzt man hinter den Betrag.

How much is it? Wie viel kostet das?

Redeabsicht:
Wenn man über den Preis einer Ware spricht, so fragt man:

Redemittel:
How much is the cap?
Wie viel kostet die Mütze?
It's one pound fifty.
Sie kostet £1.50.

Redeabsicht:
Über mehrere Sachen spricht man so:

Redemittel:
How much are the sweets?
Wie viel kosten die Bonbons?
They are eighty pence.
Sie kosten 80 p.

Ü 15.1. How much is it?

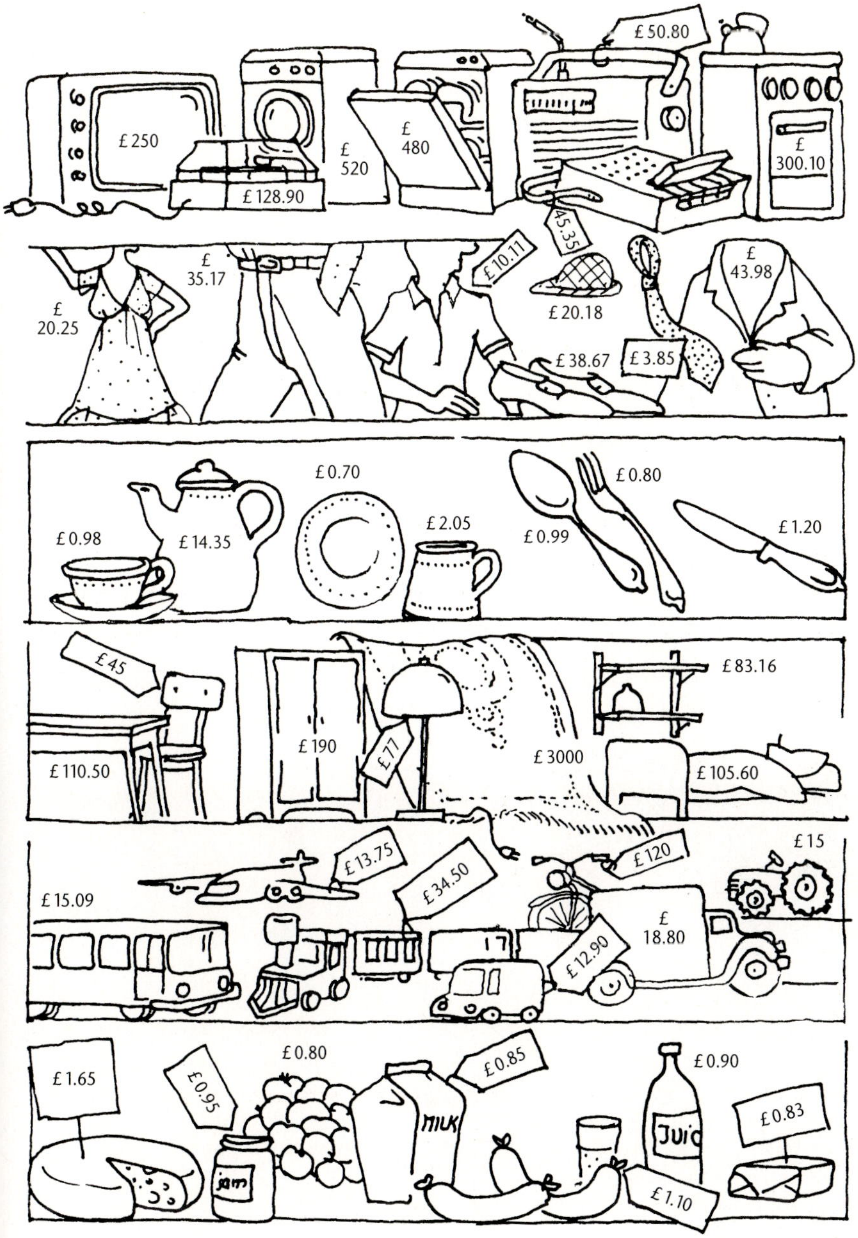

electrical goods

clothes

dishes cutlery (Geschirr und Besteck)

furniture

toys vehicles

food

It's your turn. Ask how much the things are.

Example: How much is the TV-set? It's two hundred and fifty pounds. How much are the trousers? They are thirty-five pounds seventeen pence.

Übungsziel: Läden und ihr Angebot kennen lernen; einkaufen können

roll – Brötchen
writing-pad – Schreibblock

16. Going shopping

Ü 16.1. What shop is it?

Have a look at the goods the shops sell and try to find out their names.

bread rolls biscuits cake	apples oranges tomatoes peas	sausages bacon meat	writing-pads envelopes pens exercise books	medicines toothpaste films sunglasses

______

shoes boots repairs	sugar tea household	coffee butter goods	haircut manicure	flowers plants	newspapers magazines cigarettes sweets

______

CDs drums guitars	fresh fish fish filets	teddy bears model planes toy cars kites	tennis rackets skis footballs sportswear

______

rings
watches
clocks

cheese
cornflakes
eggs

butter
soap
toothpaste

chocolate
salt
beer

coats
shirts
jackets
dresses

shoe-shop – sports shop – hairdresser's shop – chemist's shop – fishmonger – bakery – stationer's shop – jeweller's – boutique – toy shop – grocer's shop – newsagent's – greengrocer's shop – florist's shop – music store – butcher – supermarket

In English we often shorten the names of the shops.
We say ***at the newsagent's*** instead of ***at the newsagent's shop***.

Ü 16.2. Where can you buy?

Ask questions and answer them. Write them down in your exercise book.

Example:

1. Where can you buy fruit and vegetables?

At the greengrocer's.

Ü 16.3. Your favourite shops

Make a list of shops which are in your town. Describe them and use the words below. Make sentences.

name of the shop	kind of shop	what you like	what you dislike

queue – Schlange

bargain – Schnäppchen, Gelegenheitskauf

friendly assistants
better choice
fresh goods
more bargains
not expensive
fashionable
clean

crowded
queues
more expensive
too far away
old-fashioned
dirty
no quality

Example:
I think the greengrocer's shop near our house is O. K., because the goods are always fresh and the shop assistants are very friendly.

What do you buy

Die Mengenbezeichnungen werden im Englischen mit *of* gebildet. Nur bei reinen Zahlenangaben fällt das *of* weg.

a packet of tea

a box of chocolates

a bar of chocolate

a bowl of rice

a bowl of sugar

a jar of jam

a jug of water

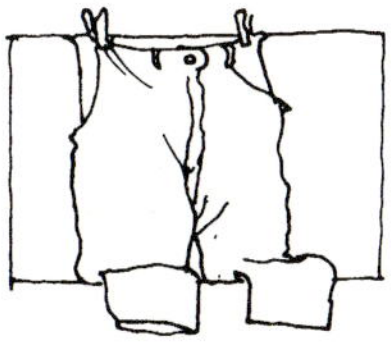
a pair of trousers

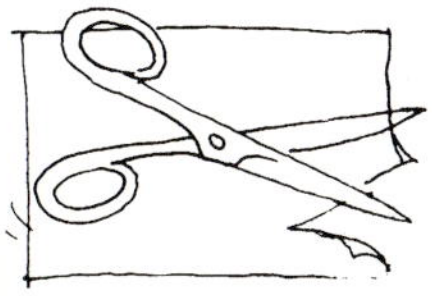
a pair of scissors

a packet of biscuits

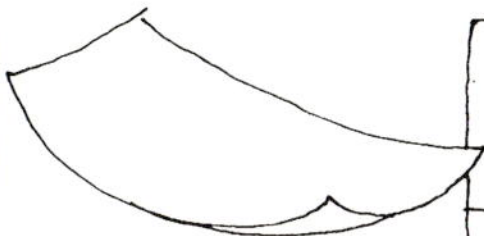
a piece of paper

a bottle of ink

a bottle of milk

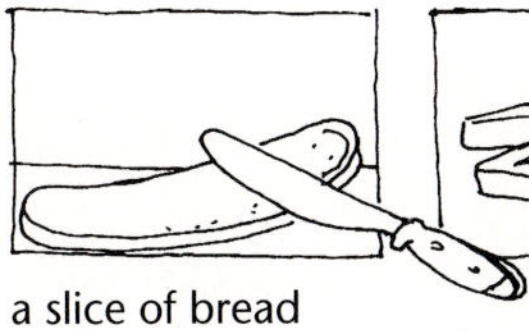
a slice of bread

a packet of chewing-gum

a glass of water

a slice of cake

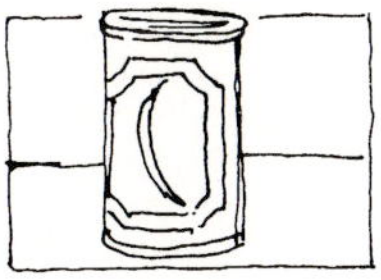
a tin of beans

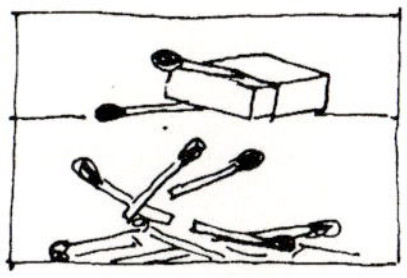
a box of matches

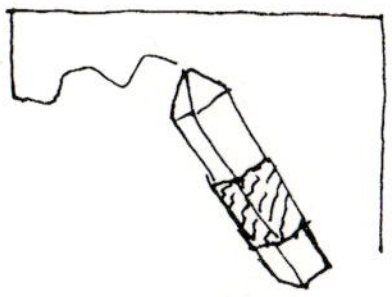
a piece of chalk

a cup of coffee
a lump of sugar

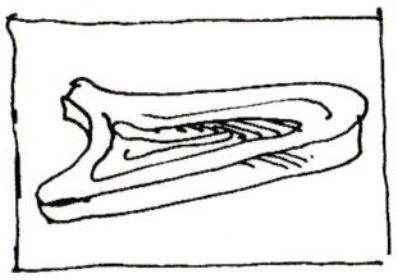
a piece of meat

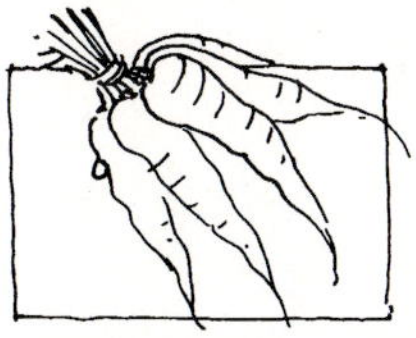
a bunch of carrots

three pounds of tomatoes

a kilo of potatoes

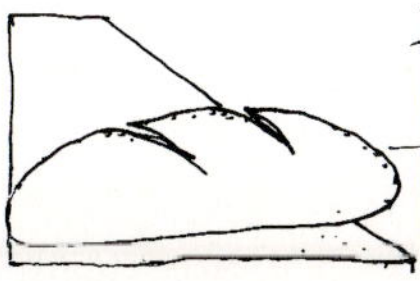
a loaf of bread

a bunch of flowers

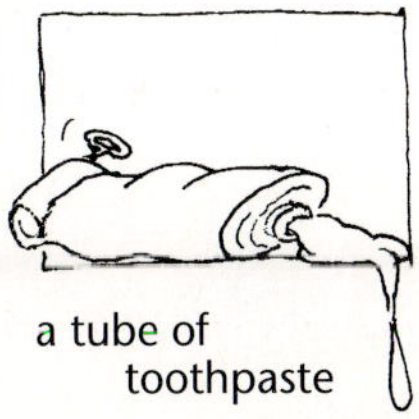
a tube of toothpaste

aber: weil es sich um reine Zahlenangaben handelt:

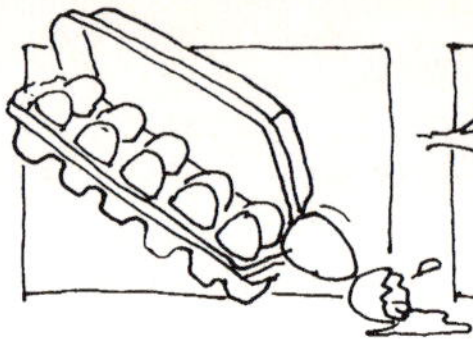

a dozen eggs

half a dozen onions

Ü 16.4. Matching exercise

Match the containers to the goods.

Example: 0O a bunch of flowers

0 a bunch	
1 	8 
2 a packet	9 
3 box	10 a pair
4 	11 a tin
5 bottle	12 
6 bar	13 a sack
7 a piece	14 a loaf

0 	
A 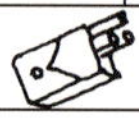	H 
B 	I 
C toothpaste	J wine
D sugar	K milk
E 	L 
F 	M tea
G jam	N chocolate

1	2	3	4	5	6	7	8	9	10	11	12	13	14
C													

Ü 16.5. Shopping list

Mary goes shopping. Prepare her shopping list.

Shopping list

two jars of jam

Ü 16.6. A story

Read the story and rewrite it in your exercise book.

It's Monday. Mrs. Smith is shopping with her daughter Anne and her son Ben in a 

. Mrs. Smith has a  in her  and she is putting the things into a trolley. What has she got in her  ? There are , 

, , and a 

.

Anne is shopping, too. She is putting  and  into a .

She is buying things for her 

.

Ben has an  in his .

"Put these toy animals into the trolley, Mummy. I'd like that , those oxen, and this funny white  for my toy farm." "Oh no, Ben, we can't take all those animals. But look at that 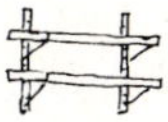 over there. There is a beautiful 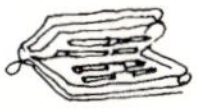 with , ,  and a  in it. You can buy that 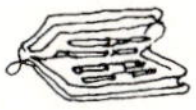. "Oh, Mummy, can't I have that  instead and then some 

?"

"No, Ben, no. You can take the  but not the other things."

Ben is very angry. Suddenly a hand touches his 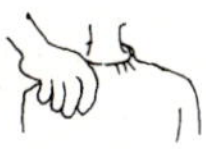. "Wait a minute, young man, can I have a look in your ?"

What to say in a shop

customer

Redeabsicht	Redemittel	
du fragst, was … kostet	*How much is …? / are …?*	
du fragst, ob … vorhanden ist	*Have you got any …? / some …?*	
du sagst, wie viel du haben willst	*I want* *Can I have* *Have you got* *I'd like*	*a packet of …* *a box of …* *a loaf of …* *half a pound of …* *three …* *a dozen …*
du sagst, dass dir etwas zu teuer ist	*It's too much.* *It's too expensive.*	
du bestätigst dem Verkäufer, dass du etwas nehmen willst	*All right.* *Lovely.* *That's fine.* *I'll take it.*	
du sagst, dass du nichts weiter haben möchtest	*That's all then.* *That's all, thank you.*	

shop assistant

Redeabsicht	Redemittel
er will wissen, was du möchtest	*What can I do for you?* *Can I help you?* *Yes, please?* *Yes, dear?*
er will wissen, wie viel du möchtest	*How much do you want?* *many* *What size?* *Half a pound or more?*

Redeabsicht	Redemittel
er will dir etwas anbieten	*It's a good buy today.* *It's a special offer today.* *It's a bargain.* *It's only ... pound today.*
er sagt, dass er etwas nicht vorrätig hat	*Sorry, I don't have any.* *Sorry, not today.*
er reicht dir etwas über die Theke	*Here you are.*
er fragt, ob du noch etwas möchtest	*Anything else?* *What else?*
er bestätigt, dass etwas davon da ist	*Yes, I have got some ...*
er nennt dir die Endsumme	*That's ... pound / pence altogether*
er fragt, wer der Nächste ist	*Who is next?* *Next please.*

shop assistant

special offer – Sonderangebot

Ü 16.7. At the grocer's

Complete the dialogue.

Shop assistant: Good morning, Miss. What can I do for you?

You: Can I ____

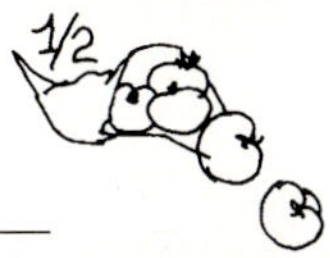

Shop assistant: All right, there you are. Anything else?

You: Yes ____

Shop assistant: Is that all you need?

You: No, I ____, too.

Shop assistant: Here you are.

You: All right, how much ____

Shop assistant: Let me see. That's £4.80.

Shop assistant: Yes, thank you, a five pound note. Here's your change: 20 pence.

You: ____

Shop assistant: Goodbye.

Ü 16.8. Shopping

In a small shop near a camping site in England there is a German lady who wants to buy some things. She doesn't speak English, so you help her.

Lady: Du kannst Englisch? Prima, bitte hilf mir doch etwas. Also, ich brauche ein Pfund Butter, eine Flasche Milch und zehn Eier.

You: A pound of ... ____________________

Lady: Frage ihn, ob er auch Fleisch und Wurst verkauft.

You: ____________________

Lady: Ah, nur Schinken und Würstchen. Gut, dann nehme ich noch ein halbes Pfund Schinken. Und frage ihn doch bitte, wo man hier Fleisch bekommt.

You: ____________________

Lady: Ach, beim Metzger im Dorf. Gut. Dann noch ein Päckchen Tee, ein halbes Pfund Kaffee und eine Flasche Orangensaft.

You: ____________________

Lady: Ach ja, und noch ein paar Süßigkeiten. Frag ihn doch bitte, was für Süßigkeiten er hat.

You: ____________________

Lady: Nur Schokolade und Kekse? Schön, dann eine Tafel Schokolade – nein, zwei. Eine ist für dich, weil du mir so schön geholfen hast.

You: ____________________

Lady: Das wär's. Frag ihn doch bitte, was das kostet.

You: ____________________

Lady: Schön. Danke für deine Hilfe – und hier ist deine Schokolade.

Ü 16.9. A funny department store

Put the things in the right departments.

department store – Kaufhaus, Warenhaus

third floor

second floor

first floor

ground floor

basement

ground floor – Erdgeschoss

basement – Keller, Untergeschoss

basement	**Food:**	**Tools:**
ground floor	**Books / Stationery:** pencils	**Pets:**
1st floor	**Ladies' Wear:**	**Men's Wear:**
2nd floor	**Radio / Television:**	**Toys / Shoes:**
3rd floor	**Children's Wear:**	**Sportswear:** racket

Übungsziel:
Einen Überblick über das englische Zeitsystem bekommen

17. Tenses

Die Form des Verbs zeigt die Zeitstufe an. Daher nennt man es im Deutschen auch Zeitwort. Im Deutschen kannst du die Zeiten relativ frei gebrauchen. Im Englischen ist der Gebrauch der Zeiten genau festgelegt. Deshalb musst du dieses Kapitel besonders sorgfältig üben.

Man unterscheidet verschiedene **Zeitstufen**:

past tense Vergangenheit — ***present tense*** Gegenwart — ***future*** Zukunft

Vorvergangenheit ***past perfect*** — Vorgegenwart ***present perfect***

Um die Zeitstufen deutlich zu machen, wird die Form des Verbs verändert. Wie im Deutschen auch musst du drei Verbformen lernen, um die verschiedenen Zeiten bilden zu können. Es gibt viele regelmäßige Verben, bei denen diese Formen immer gleich konstruiert werden. Bei den unregelmäßigen Verben musst du die Verbformen auswendig lernen.

Die erste Form ist der Infinitiv des Verbs, *the* ***infinitive****: ask.*
Daraus werden die Formen im Präsens, im ***present***, gebildet. Sie heißen alle gleich – außer in der 3. Person Singular. Dort wird ein *-s* angehängt:

> *I ask, you ask, he / she / it asks, we ask, you ask, they ask.*

Die zweite Form ist das Imperfekt, *the* ***past tense***. Bei regelmäßigen Verben wird an den Infinitiv einfach *-ed* angehängt: *asked.*
Hier haben alle Personen die gleiche Form:

> *I asked, you asked, he / she / it asked, we asked, you asked, they asked.*

Die dritte Form des Verbs ist das Partizip, das ***past participle.***
Bei regelmäßigen Verben wird auch hier einfach *-ed* an den Infinitiv angehängt: *asked.*
Diese Form brauchst du, um das *present perfect* und das *past perfect* zu bilden.

Beim *present perfect* verwendet man *have / has* und das *past participle:*

> *I have asked, you have asked, he / she / it has asked, we have asked, you have asked, they have asked.*

Beim *past perfect* verwendet man die Vergangenheitsform von *have*, nämlich *had* und das *past participle.*
Auch hier haben alle Personen die gleiche Form:

> *I had asked, you had asked, he / she / it had asked, we had asked, you had asked, they had asked.*

So sehen also die Formen der regelmäßigen Verben aus:

ask, asked, asked
help, helped, helped
watch, watched, watched

Hier einige unregelmäßige Verben:

go, went, gone
write, wrote, written
get, got, got

Read the following sentences and try to follow the tenses:

Yesterday Peter got a letter, which his friend had written the day before.
Today Peter posts the answer which he has just written to Tom. — *to post – zur Post bringen*
Tomorrow Tom will get Peter's answer.

Plusquamperfekt Vorvergangenheit **past perfect**	Imperfekt / Präteritum Vergangenheit **past tense**	Perfekt Vorgegenwart **present perfect**	Präsens Gegenwart **present tense**	Futur Zukunft **future**
Monday	Tuesday	Wednesday in the morning	Wednesday at noon	Thursday
had + past participle	past tense form of the verb: *-ed* or irregular	*has / have* + past participle	present tense form of the verb; 3rd person singular: + *s*	*will* + infinitive
				Tomorrow Tom will get Peter's answer
			Today Peter posts the answer,	
		which he has just written to Tom.		
	Yesterday Peter got a letter,			
which his friend had written the day before.				

Übungsziel:
Die einfache Form der Gegenwart benutzen können

18. Present Tense

Das ***simple present*** wird bei Tätigkeits- und Vorgangsverben benutzt,

i

wenn etwas wiederholt wird oder immer wieder passiert. Es gibt Wörter, die das anzeigen: *often – always – usually – every …*

My father gets up at six every morning.

I always play tennis on Wednesdays.

Hier geht es um Gewohnheiten.

wenn etwas immer so ist:

The sun rises in the east.

The Thames flows into the North Sea.

Hier geht es um allgemein gültige Tatsachen.

wenn Handlungen aufeinander folgen:

Shirley wakes up, yawns, stretches her arms, gets out of bed and goes to the bathroom.

Hier wird die Abfolge von Handlungen betont. Du findest diese Form bei Erzählungen, Sportberichten und Gebrauchsanweisungen.

Englische Verben hatten ursprünglich wie im Deutschen für jede Person eine eigene Endung. Heute hat nur noch die 3. Person im Präsens die Endung *-s*.

mother – she –
Peter – he –
the cat – it

to the station

we – they –
you – I

the room

Rules of writing

1. An die Grundform des Verbs wird ein *-s* angehängt:
   to ask – he asks / to write – she writes / to happen – it happens

2. Endet das Verb auf einen Zischlaut, so wird *-es* angehängt:
   to watch – he watches / to fetch – he fetches / to miss – it misses

3. Endet ein Verb auf *-y* und es geht ein Konsonant voraus, so wird *-y* zu *-ie* und dann wird ein *-s* angehängt:
   to fly – it flies / to hurry – she hurries

4. Geht bei einem Verb, das auf *-y* endet, ein Vokal voraus, dann bleibt das *-y* und es wird einfach ein *-s* angehängt:
   to play – she plays / to say – he says

Ü 18.1. The 3rd person singular verb machine

1. You say — he / she says
2. they fly — ____________
3. we get — ____________
4. I fetch — ____________
5. you do — ____________
6. I buy — ____________
7. they catch — ____________
8. we cook — ____________
9. you hurry — ____________
10. I go — ____________
11. you kiss — ____________

Signal words

Folgende Signalwörter zeigen dir an, dass du *simple present tense* verwenden musst:

often	oft	*every day*	jeden Tag
always	immer	*never*	niemals
sometimes	manchmal	*usually*	gewöhnlich
seldom	selten		

Ü 18.2. What do you do?

Write sentences about the children and about yourself.

	Fred	**Susan**	**Peter**	**You**
CDs	sometimes with friends	never on Mondays	every day	
books	often	sometimes	seldom	
football	seldom in the school team	never	never	
housework	never	seldom	every day	
TV	usually in the evening	sometimes pop shows	often action movies	

Example: Fred sometimes listens to CDs with friends.

Ü 18.3. Jobs at home

Look at the pictures and write down what Fred does at home every day, every week, every month, seldom or never.

doing the cooking – washing the dishes – cleaning the floor – doing the shopping – washing the car – setting the table – watering the flowers – cleaning the shoes – making breakfast – emptying the dustbin – making the beds – washing the clothes – tidying the bedroom

Example: Fred does the cooking every day. He cleans the shoes every month.

Ü 18.4. General facts: The solar system

Read the following text and fill in the right words in the picture on page 129.

to spin – um sich drehen
axis – Achse

There are nine planets in our solar system. They all go round the sun. Our earth is one of the planets of the sun. The earth goes round the sun once a year. At the same time it spins round and round on its own axis once in twenty-four hours. For the people on earth it seems as if the sun rises in the east and sets in the west. Some planets have satellites. A satellite goes round a planet. The earth has one satellite. It's the moon. The moon goes round the earth once in twenty-eight days.

Ü 18.5. A gentleman

What can you say about a gentleman. Write down sentences.

Example: His name is David. He is thirty years old.

name	David	30	to be 30 years old
to live in	London	GB	to come from
to live in	flat	6 rooms	to have 6 rooms
to work as a	teacher	big school	to work in a
to speak	English	German	to speak
to be	married	4 children	to have
to like	football	Italy	
	fishing	boxing	
		TV	to hate
to play	tennis	beer	
		warm milk	
to collect	stamps		
	records		

Ü 18.6. Jobs and what to do on the job

Look at the picture and write the names of the jobs.

technician – car mechanic – nurse – electrician – dentist – plumber – cook – gardener – veterinarian – painter – psychiatrist – dock worker – carpenter – secretary – artist – fireman – actor – housewife – chimney sweep – builder – engineer – butcher – bus driver – clerk – shop assistant – doctor – farmer – waitress – teacher – manager

Ü 18.7. Who does what?

Build sentences. Write in your exercise book.

teaches.
works on a ship.
does the housework.
works in the fields.
works in a factory.
takes people from one place to another.
paints houses and doors.
types letters.
brings you the food in a restaurant.
repairs cars.
flies new planes.
finds out what's the matter with you when you're ill.
cleans the chimney.
must be very good at playing football.
stops cars which go too fast.
drives a bus.
cleans other people's houses.
helps you when you've got a toothache.
makes meals.
sells things in a shop.
helps the doctor.
repairs ships.
brings the letters.
makes furniture.
makes bread and cakes.

A …
is a person
who …

Example: A baker is a person who makes bread and cakes.

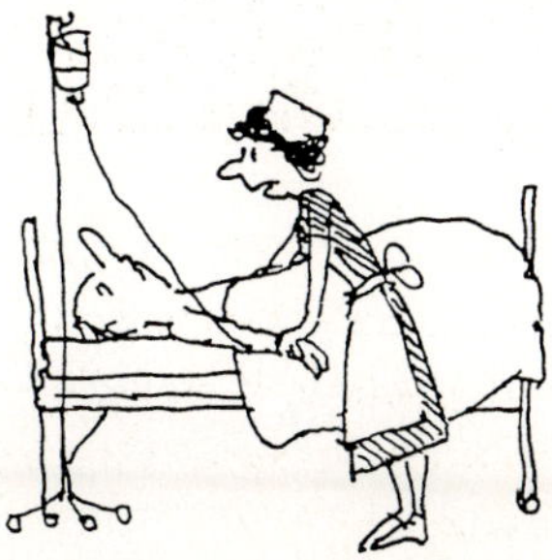

Ü 18.8. Your ideal job

Over to you. Answer the questions. Mark your answers. Look up and add the points. You will find out your ideal job.

yes / no

1 Are you patient?

yes / no

2 Do you like to be alone?

yes / no

3 Are you calm?

yes / no

4 Do you like to help people?

yes / no

5 Are you energetic?

yes / no

6 Are you artistic?

yes / no

7 Are you well-organised?

yes / no

8 Do you like fresh air?

yes / no

9 Are you good with your hands?

yes / no

10 Do you like sport?

yes / no

11 Do you hate noise?

yes / no

12 Do you like phoning?

yes / no

13 Do you like to travel?

yes / no

14 Do you like children?

yes / no

15 Do you hate the dark?

yes / no

16 Do you like blood?

yes / no

17 Do you like maths?

yes / no

18 Do you like music?

yes / no

19 Do you like animals?

yes / no

20 Do you like to talk?

0–55 points

teacher | doctor | nurse | psychiatrist | policeman | vet

56–90 points

technician | artist | bank clerk | mechanic | hairdresser | chef

91–120 points

photographer | air steward(ess) | fireman | shop assistant | actor | secretary

Score

Q	Yes	No
1	2	0
2	5	0
3	2	0
4	2	4
5	10	4
6	5	4
7	10	3
8	5	3
9	5	2
10	10	1
11	1	10
12	10	4
13	10	1
14	2	5
15	2	4
16	5	2
17	5	2
18	5	7
19	2	5
20	10	5

Ü 18.9. One thing after the other

Look at the pictures. Describe what Fred does every morning.

Every morning Fred wakes up at seven o'clock.

Ü 18.10. Waking up in the morning

Write down how Fred wakes up the boy. Write in your exercise book.
Use the following singal words:
first – then – after – finally

This list will help you:

offer sausage – hen lay an egg – sleeping boy wake up – wag tail – make hole in fishtank– bell ring – egg fall into net – water pour down – revolver fire

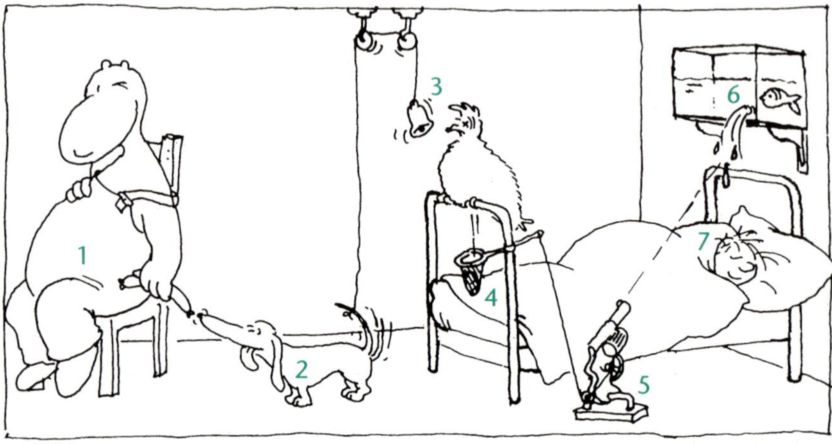

First Fred offers a sausage to his dog.

Ü 18.11. Over to you

Do you

	Yes, always.	Yes, usually.	Yes, often.	Yes, sometimes.	No, not usually.	No, not very often.	No, never.
wake up without an alarm clock?							
listen to the radio before you go to school?							
drink tea or coffee in the morning?							
do your homework at school?							
feel nervous when you meet new people?							
borrow books from the library?							
clean your shoes yourself?							
drink beer?							
go jogging?							

19. Simple Past Tense

Übungsziel:
Die Verbformen der Vergangenheit kennen lernen und benutzen können

Yesterday ...

I watched TV.
You washed the car.
He did his homework.
She ate three apples.
It rained all day.
We bought funny shirts.
You played with your dogs.
They helped their mother.

Did I watch TV?
Did you wash the car?
Did he do his homework?
Did she eat three apples?
Did it rain all day?
Did we buy funny shirts?
Did you play with your dogs?
Did they help their mother?

What did I watch?
Where did you wash the car?
Where did he do his homework?
Why did she eat three apples?
Why did it rain all day?
Where did we buy funny shirts?
When did you play with your dogs?
Why did they help their mother?

I didn't watch TV.
You didn't wash the car.
He didn't do his homework.
She didn't eat three apples.
It didn't rain all day.
We didn't buy funny shirts.
You didn't play with your dogs.
They didn't help their mother.

Was I at school?
Were you at school?
Was he at school?
Was she at school?
Was it at school?
Were we at school?
Were you at school?
Were they at school?

I wasn't at school.
You weren't at school.
He wasn't at school.
She wasn't at school.
It wasn't at school.
We weren't at school.
You weren't at school.
They weren't at school.

Learn the forms by heart!

Das *past tense* wird verwendet, wenn der Sprecher über einen Vorgang in der Vergangenheit berichtet. Er denkt dabei an einen bestimmten Zeitpunkt bzw. einen abgeschlossenen Vorgang, der in der Vergangenheit liegt bzw. dort beendet wurde. Zeitpunkt oder Zeitraum stehen nicht in Verbindung mit der Gegenwart. Durch eine Zeitbestimmung oder ein *signal word* wird dieser Zeitpunkt oder Zeitraum ausdrücklich gekennzeichnet.

When?

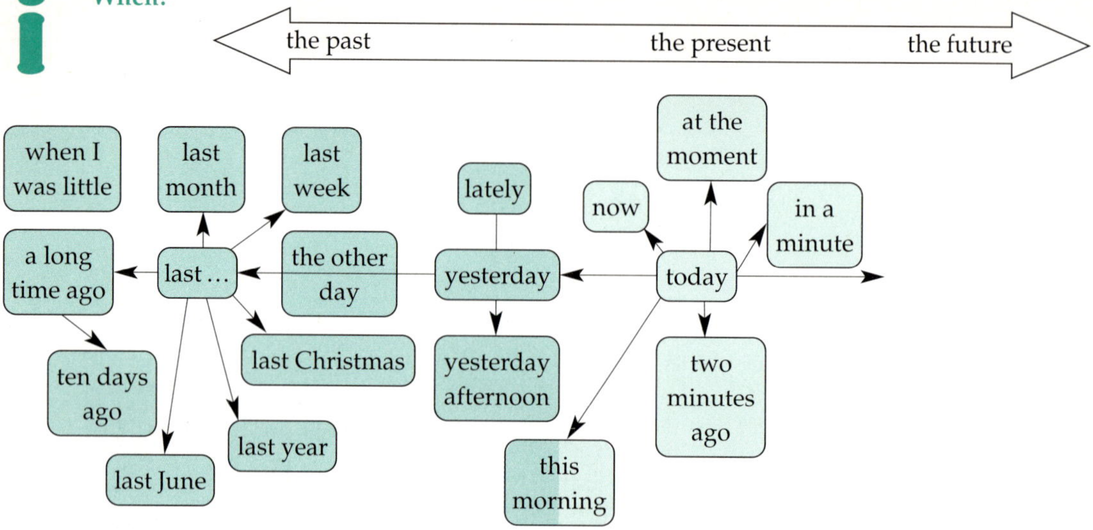

Das *past tense* wird gebildet, indem man an den Infinitiv eines Verbs *-ed* anhängt. Die so entstandene Form ist in allen Personen gleich. Die 3. Person Singular hat also nicht – wie im *present tense* – das *-s* angehängt.

Natürlich gibt es nicht nur regelmäßige Verben, sondern – wie im Deutschen – auch unregelmäßige, die du lernen musst. Im Verzeichnis der unregelmäßigen Verben auf S. 169 f. ist das *past* die zweite Form.

Rules of writing

Auch bei den regelmäßigen Verben kannst du nicht immer *-ed* anhängen. Du musst einige Schreibregeln beachten:

-y wird zu *-i*	Endet ein Verb auf *-y* und steht davor ein Konsonant, dann wird das *-y* zu *-i*. Im *simple past* enden diese Verben also auf *-ied*. Nach einem Vokal bleibt das *-y* allerdings erhalten.	*cry – cried* *The baby cried all night.* *play – played* *The girl played tennis.*
Wegfall des stummen *-e*	Endet ein Verb im Infinitiv auf einem stummen *-e*, dann wird im *simple past* nur noch ein *-d* angehängt.	*smile – smiled* *Fred smiled at me.* *use – used* *I always used my biro.*
Endkonsonanten-verdoppelung	Ein einfacher Endkonsonant wird verdoppelt, wenn der Buchstabe davor ein kurzer betonter Vokal ist. Erst dann wird *-ed* angehängt.	*plan – planned* *My brother planned a tour.*

Ü 19.1. What a wonderful weekend

Write down what the pupils did last weekend.

I washed my bike.

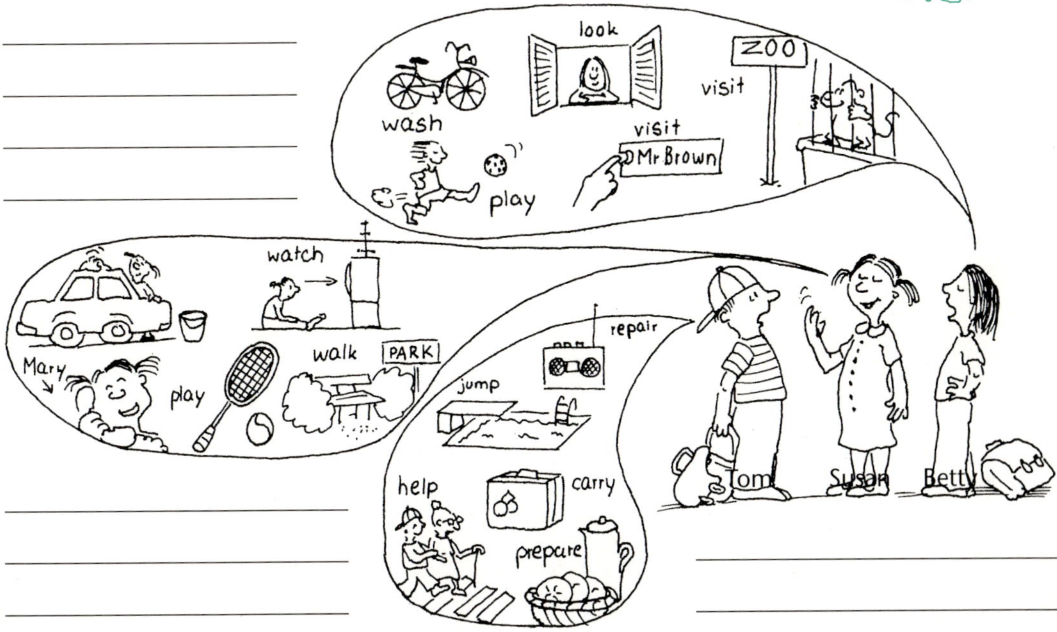

Ü 19.2. The bank raid

Fill in the past tense form of the verbs.

Yesterday there was a bank raid on the Bank of London in Darktown. A man with a black stocking over his head ______________ (rob) the bank. Two twelve year old girls, who ______________ (watch) this from a shop nearby ______________ (phone) the police.

bank raid – Banküberfall

When the police car ______________ (stop) in front of the bank the thief ______________ (try) to run away. On his way he ______________ (drop) the bag with the money. At that moment one of the policemen ______________ (grab) the thief and ______________ (arrest) him.

grab – packen, (sich) schnappen

Ü 19.3. Past tense forms

Now look at the forms of the verbs in the last two exercises again and make a list in your exercise book.

infinitive	simple past	infinitive	simple past
wash	washed	play	played

Ü 19.4. Fred and the black cat

Look at the pictures and put them into the correct order.

3														

switch on the light

go upstairs

wake up

get into bed

take off his dressing gown

open the door

see a cat outside the window

open the bedroom door

hear a noise

put on his dressing gown

switch off the light

go to sleep

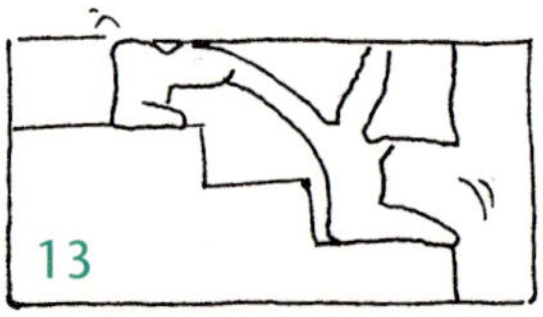

go downstairs

listen at the door

get out of bed

Write the story in your exercise book. Begin like this:

Fred woke up. He heard a noise. He switched on the light ...

If you don't know the past tense form of some verbs look at the list of irregular verbs on pages 169 / 170.

Now group the verbs in regular and irregular forms.

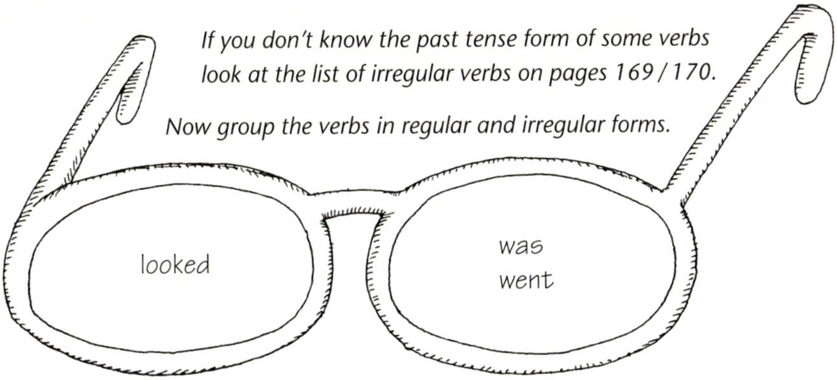

Ü 19.5. A ghost story

Complete the story. Fill in the blanks.

It ___was___ (be) night.

There ____________ (be) a big yellow ____________  in the sky.

Jane and I ____________ (be) looking at an old ____________. 

"What a strange place", Jane ____________ (say). "Let's go inside".

"No", I ____________ (answer). "I don't want to. I don't like this place.

It frightens me." "Don't be stupid", Jane ____________ (say).

Then Jane ____________ (open) the ____________  and

____________ (walk) inside.

I ____________ (follow) her after a few seconds. It ____________ (be)

very ____________  inside. I ____________ (can not) see Jane.

Suddenly there ____________ (be) a ____________. 

"Jane", I ____________ (shout), "Where are you? Don't leave me alone."

Then I ____________ (feel) a cold ____________  on my

____________. 

I ___________ (turn) and ___________ (see) a horrible

___________. 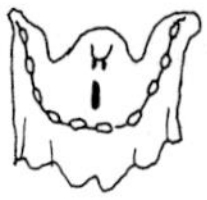

It ___________ (be) a man without a head.

He ___________ (be) holding a ___________. 

"Don't hurt me", I ___________ (shout). Then two more ghosts

___________ (appear). A lady with ___________  on her dress

and a ___________. 

"Do you know my name?" ___________ (ask) the lady ghost.

"No, Miss", I ___________ (say). "I'm Princess Vampire. I don't like visitors

in my house. I kill them."

"Wake up, wake up! You are shouting in your sleep." Jane ___________

(be) shaking my arms. "What's wrong? Are you having a bad dream?"

skeleton – Skelett

Ü 19.6. A crossword puzzle

Can you fill in the past tense forms in the crossword puzzle? Be careful, these are irregular verbs. If you don't know the past tense forms look them up in the list on pages 169 / 170.

Across:

1 to bite
11 to run
16 to dig
25 to sell
31 to feel
3 to bring
12 to choose
17 to draw
26 to meet
34 to keep
7 to lead
13 to throw
18 to hold
28 to shoot
35 to sleep
10 to drink
15 to say
23 to understand
29 to think
36 to sit

Down:

1 to break
5 to forget
9 to tell
18 to hide
22 to go
30 to teach
2 to light
6 to sing
12 to catch
19 to lie
24 to shake
31 to fall
3 to begin
7 to leave
14 to ride
20 to lose
27 to buy
32 to lay
4 to give
8 to grow
15 ~~to shrink~~
21 to fight
28 to speak

Questions in the past tense

Fragen im *simple past* bildest du genau so wie im *present tense*. Du stellst dem Verb lediglich die *past tense form* von *to do* voran – nämlich *did*. Oder du setzt die Form von *to be* oder von einem anderen Hilfsverb in die *past tense form*.

Die Vergangenheit ist durch das *did* oder die *past tense form* eines anderen Hilfsverbs bereits ausgedrückt. Das Vollverb steht deshalb immer im Infinitiv.

Für alle Personen im Singular und im Plural ist die Form des Hilfsverbs und die des Vollverbs immer gleich.

Singular	1st		*I*		
	2nd	*Did*	*you*	*arrive*	*on time* ?
	3rd		*he*		
			she		
			it		
Plural	1st		*we*		
	2nd	*Did*	*you*	*arrive*	*on time* ?
	3rd		*they*		

▲ Hilfsverb *did* immer gleich

▲ Vollverb immer im Infinitiv

Did und Grundform ist die Norm.
Nach *did* steht nie die *past tense* Form.

Ü 19.7. Your weekend

Look at the pictures. Ask questions and give the answers. If possible work with a partner and use the chart below.

A What was your weekend like?
  B It was ...

A What did you do on ...
  B I ... and then I ... There was a ... on ...

A Did you ...?
  B Yes, I did. / No, I didn't.

A Was it nice?
  B Yes, it was. It was ... / No, it wasn't. It was ...

Ü 19.8. Going on a bike tour

One summer day Mary and Jennifer decided to go on a bike tour. They went by train to Fairlop Station, took their bikes and walked back to the road. Mary had a plan. Can you follow the route they took?

1. Along the footpath, over the bridge to visit the castle. Jennifer took photos.
2. Past the castle through a tunnel, past some cliffs to a beach. Both girls had a swim there.
3. A short ride to a wood for a picnic and a look at the harbour.
4. Back to the road, over a bridge to some crossroads, then right along a main road to look at a church.
5. Straight back to the road and a break at a restaurant for an ice cream and fish and chips. Girls are always hungry.
6. From the restaurant they turned right, rode their bikes to the crossroads, across a bridge straight ahead, took the first turning on the left and then the first turning on the right until they reached a farm. The farmer let them look at the animals.
7. After that they rode along the footpath to the pond. Mary caught a fish but threw it back again.
8. They crossed the road, followed the footpath past the church (more photos), crossed another road, still following the footpath.
9. Near the little wood they paddled in a stream and ate the rest of their sandwiches. Then happy but tired they crossed the road to Barkingside Station. It had been a very nice outing.

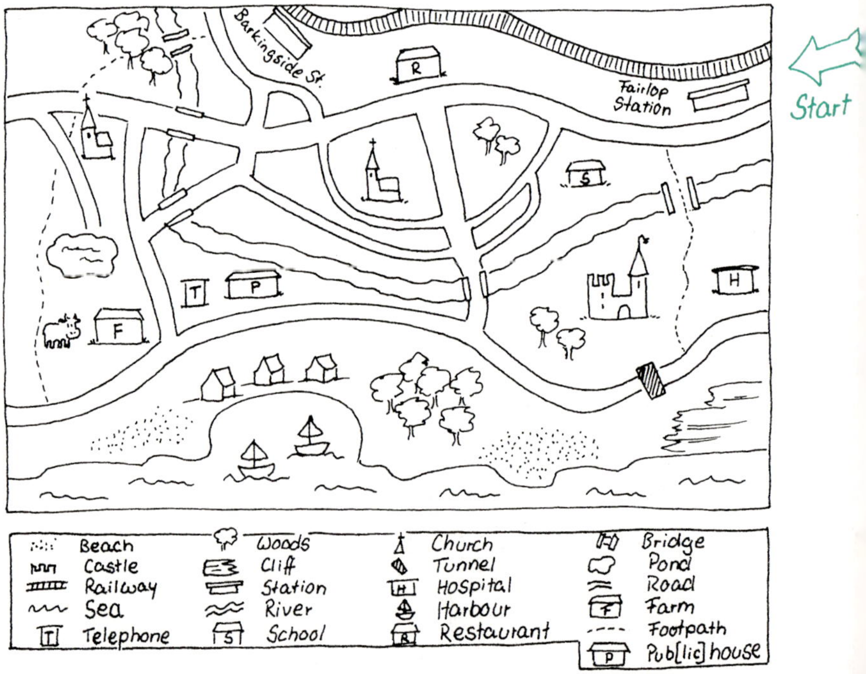

Ü 19.9. Fred is back

Fred is back from his holiday. He tells his friends about it. Use the phrases below and think of more.

the bed – the room – the sandwiches – the TV programmes – the weather – the shops – the waiters – the beach – the drinks – the people – the museums – the water

quite good – lousy – not bad – super – expensive – friendly – large – too small – fantastic – boring – beautiful – perfect – terribly dirty

Example:
A: You're back, Fred, that's nice. Tell us about your hotel. How was the food?
F: Oh, well, the food was terrible. Almost every day the potatoes were burnt.

Ü 19.10. Your holiday

Did you go on holiday last year? Write about your holiday and use the notes.

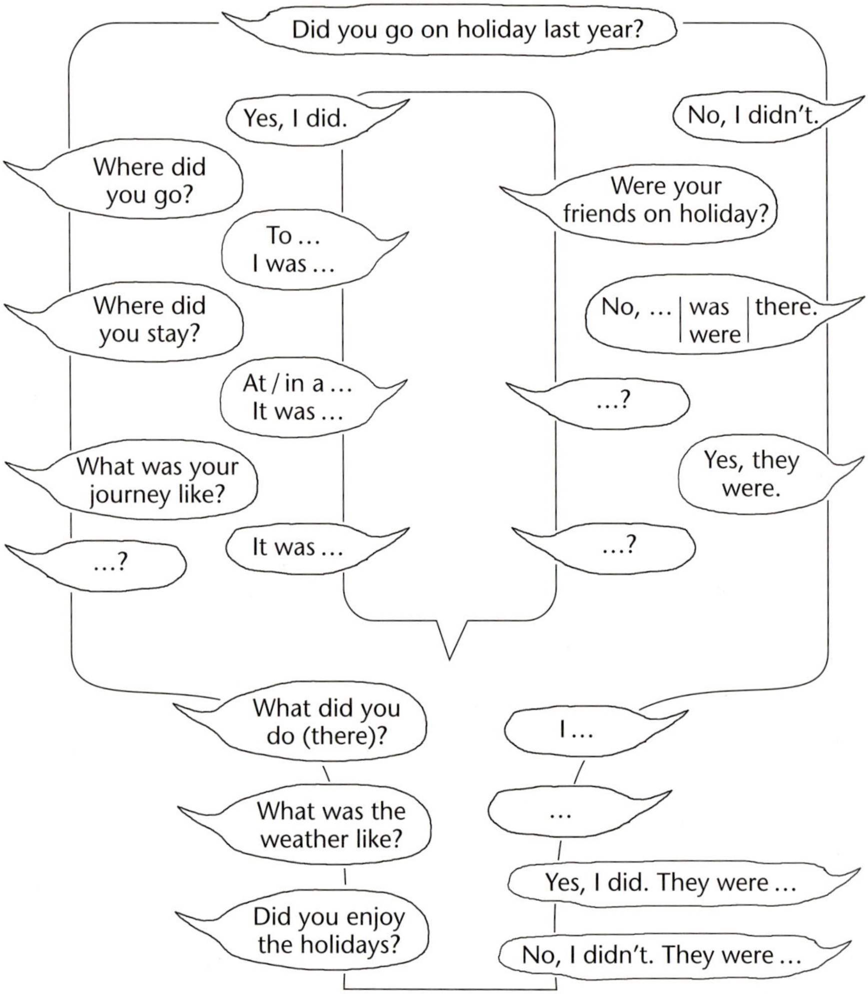

Did you go on holiday?
Make notes about your holiday.

journey · not bad · interesting · people · cold · campsite · hotel room · weather · terrible

Didn't you go on holiday?
What did you do in your holidays?
Make notes.

visited … · rainy · weather · sunny · books · went … · boring

Start like this:

I spent my last holiday in … I went to … I was with my … We had … The weather was …

Ü 19.11. Your own life story

This is a quiz about your own past, so you might need to check most of the answers with your parents.

1. What did you weigh when you were born?

2. What day of the week were you born on?

3. Did you use to cry a lot when you were a baby?

4. What used to be your favourite food when you were very little. Describe two or three things.

5. Did you use to have a nickname in your family when you were very small?

6. Who used to take you to school when you were little?

7. What used to be your favourite toy when you were little?

8. Who used to be your best friend when you first started school?

9. Who used to be your favourite character in a book when you were young?

10. What was your first word?

11. When did you first walk?

12. Did you use to be afraid of anyone in particular when you were very young?

Now write down your own life story in your exercise book.

It all started like this: I was born at exactly … on … When I was born my weight was … My parents lived in … Later we moved to … As a baby I didn't cry a lot … As a child my hobbies were … I was afraid of … I had … I went to primary school in … The colour of my hair was …

Ü 19.12. The frog prince – a fairy tale

Write the past tense forms of the verbs in your exercise book. Don't forget to add the numbers!

once upon a time – es war einmal

Once upon a time, there **1** (live) a King who **2** (have) seven beautiful daughters, the youngest **3** (be) the most beautiful. The princess **4** (have) one favourite thing among all her toys. It **5** (be) a golden ball. She **6** (spend) many hours throwing it up into the air and catching it.

Near the King's castle **7** (be) a big forest. Under a big tree there **8** (be) a deep dark pool. The princess often **9** (go) there to play by herself. She **10** (use) to run about near the pool, throwing up her golden ball and catching it.

however – hier: jedoch

loss – Verlust

One day however, when the princess **11** (throw) her ball, it **12** (fall) into the deep pool with a loud splash. The princess **13** (begin) to cry. And the more she **14** (think) about the loss of her favourite toy, the louder she **15** (cry).

nearby – in der Nähe

edge – Kante

As the princess **16** (weep) she **17** (hear) a voice saying, "Why do you weep, young princess?" The princess **18** (look) up to see who **19** (be) speaking to her. She **20** (can not) see anyone nearby. There **21** (be) only a frog sitting at the edge of the pool. So she **22** (say) to the frog: "I'm crying because my beautiful golden ball has fallen into this deep pool."

jewellery – Schmuck

"Do not cry", **23** (say) the frog, "I can help you. What will you give me if I find your ball for you?" "I will give you anything you wish for getting my ball", **24** (answer) the princess, "You can have my clothes or jewellery or even my golden crown, if only you will find my golden ball." "I do not want your clothes or your golden crown", **25** (say) the frog. "I want you to let me be your friend and play with you. I want to sit beside you at the table, eat from your golden plate and drink from your golden cup. I want to sleep in your bed beside you. If you will promise me these things", the frog **26** (go) on, "I'll dive into the deep pool and find your golden ball. Do you promise?"

promise – versprechen

however – trotzdem

The princess **27** (think) that the frog **28** (be) talking a lot of nonsense. However she **29** (want) her golden ball very much. So she **30** (say): "Yes, I will promise all that you ask, if only you will find my golden ball for me."

to turn one's back to sb. – jmd. den Rücken zukehren

At these words the frog **31** (dive) into the pool. And soon **32** (come) swimming up again with the golden ball in his mouth. He **33** (throw) the ball onto the grass. The princess **34** (be) happy to see her favourite plaything once again. She **35** (pick) it up and **36** (laugh) as she **37** (throw) it into the air and **38** (catch) it again and again. Then she **39** (turn) her back on the frog and the pool and **40** (run) away towards her father's castle.

"Wait for me, wait for me!", **41** (call) the poor frog. "I can't run as fast as you can!" And he **42** (hop) along behind the princess. But she **43** (do not) turn round but just **44** (keep) on running.

but – hier: sondern

The next day, the young princess **45** (be) sitting at dinner with the king, her men and the other princesses. As she **46** (eat) from her little golden plate, the frog **47** (come) into the great hall. He **48** (jump) from step to step up the staircase. When he **49** (get) to the top, he **50** (knock) on the door of the dining room. "Youngest princess, open the door for me", he **51** (cry). The princess **52** (run) to the door to see who **53** (be) calling to her. When she **54** (see) that it **55** (be) the frog, she **56** (be) afraid. She **57** (close) the door quickly and **58** (go) back to her place at the dining table.

The king **59** (see) that his daughter **60** (be) afraid. "My child, why are you afraid?" he **61** (ask). "Is there a giant outside the door who wishes to carry you away?" "Oh no, dear father", **62** (answer) the princess. "There is no giant, only a horrible, slimy frog." "What does the frog want with you?" **63** (ask) the king. Then the princess **64** (tell) her father what had happened the day before. "I **65** (promise) him that he **66** (can) live with me", she **67** (say), "but I never **68** (think) he would come far from the pool."

giant – Riese

Just then another knock **69** (be) heard on the door and a voice **70** (cry) out:

"Youngest princess, hear me call.
Remember you **71** (loose) your golden ball,
as you **72** (play) by yourself beside the pool.
I **73** (dive) into the water cool,
and your ball I **74** (find) and **75** (return) to you.
Now please remember your promise true,
to take me along to live with you."

"When a promise is made it must be kept", **76** (say) the king to his daughter. "Go and open the door." The youngest princess **77** (go) and **78** (open) the door. As she **79** (return) to her chair, the frog **80** (hop) behind her. When she **81** (sit) down, the frog **82** (say) "Put me on the table beside you, please." The princess **83** (do not) want to, but her father **84** (tell) her to do so. When the frog **85** (be) on the table, he **86** (say) to the princess: "Please push your little golden plate nearer to me". The princess **87** (do) so but very unwillingly. She barely **88** (touch) her food. The frog however **89** (enjoy) every bite he **90** (eat).

unwillingly – widerwillig
barely – kaum

When he had finished eating, the frog **91** (turn) to the princess and **92** (say): "Now, I'm tired. Please take me to your room and we will go to sleep." At that moment the princess **93** (burst) into tears. She **94** (do not) like to touch the cold frog and she **95** (can not) bear to think of him lying be-

to burst into tears – in Tränen ausbrechen

side her in her own bed. Then the king **96** (grow) angry and **97** (speak) sternly to his daughter. "If someone helps you when you are in trouble," he **98** (say), "you cannot afterwards turn your back on him. Take the frog with you to your room." So the princess **99** (have) to pick up the frog and take him to her room. She **100** (put) him in a corner of her room, as far away from her bed as possible. Then she **101** (get) into her silken bed and **102** (turn) her back on him. Once more the frog **103** (speak) up. "I'm tired, too", he **104** (say), "I want to sleep beside you. Please lift me up."

sternly – streng
to be in trouble – in Schwierigkeiten sein

Again the princess **105** (begin) to weep. "If you do not lift me into your bed", the frog **106** (go) on, "I shall have to tell the king, your father." The princess **107** (know) she **108** (have) no choice. So she **109** (pick) up the frog, **110** (climb) back into bed and **111** (put) him on the silken pillow beside her.

choice – Wahl

No sooner had she done so than the frog **112** (turn) into a handsome prince! He **113** (have) a kind face and **114** (smile) gently at the princess. Then he **115** (tell) her how he had been turned into a frog. The spell could only be broken if a beautiful princess would take him, eat with him and sleep with him. The prince **116** (tell) the princess how he had often watched her playing with her golden ball in the forest and how he had fallen in love with her. "Dear princess, will you marry me?" he **117** (ask).

no sooner – hier: gerade als
handsome – gut aussehend (v. a. Männer)
gently – freundlich
spell – hier: Zauber

to fall in love with sb. – sich in jmd. verlieben

The princess **118** (look) into his kind face and then hand-in-hand they **119** (go) to tell the king what had happened.

Some time later, the prince and the princess **120** (be) married and they **121** (live) happily together ever after.

ever after – hier: bis ans Ende ihrer Tage

20. The Present Perfect Tense

Übungsziel:
Das present perfect bilden und es gebrauchen können

Das *present perfect* entspricht von den Formen her etwa dem deutschen Perfekt. Im Gebrauch und in der Bedeutung weicht es jedoch häufig stark ab.

Im Deutschen wird das Perfekt mit den Hilfsverben „haben“ oder „sein“ und dem Partizip Perfekt gebildet. Im Englischen gebraucht man immer *have* oder *has* und das *past participle*. Das *past participle* ist die 3. Form des Verbs, die du in Grammatiken, Wörterbüchern oder auch in der Tabelle auf S. 169f. findest.

Die Formen

Singular	1st	*I have opened*	ich habe geöffnet
	2nd	*you have waited*	du hast gewartet
	3rd	*he has stopped* *she has written* *it has begun*	er hat angehalten sie hat geschrieben es hat angefangen
Plural	1st	*we have asked*	wir haben gefragt
	2nd	*you have lost*	ihr habt verloren
	3rd	*they have arrived*	sie sind angekommen

Um eine Frage zu bilden, musst du – wie gewohnt – die Form von *have*, das Hilfsverb also, voranstellen:
Have you waited?

Um die Verneinung zu bilden, wird das Hilfsverb verneint.
I have not waited. Die Kurzform lautet: *I haven't waited.*

The past participle

Das *past participle* von regelmäßigen Verben kannst du bilden, indem du *-ed* an den Infinitiv des Verbs anhängst. Es wird also genauso gebildet wie die *past tense form* von regelmäßigen Verben und auch so ausgesprochen. Für das *past participle* gelten dann ebenfalls die gleichen Schreib- und Ausspracheregeln.

Das *past participle* von unregelmäßigen Verben kannst du nicht ableiten. Du musst die Formen einfach so lange üben, bis du sie auswendig kannst und automatisch richtig machst.

Auf der nächsten Seite findest du noch einmal eine Zusammenstellung von einigen regelmäßigen und wichtigen unregelmäßigen Verbformen. Lies die Verben laut und ergänze beim *past participle* verschiedene Personen und *have* bzw. *has*. Wenn du unsicher bist, schaust du am besten auf dieser Seite noch einmal nach!

regular verbs

infinitive	past	past participle
stop	stopped	stopped
telephone	telephoned	telephoned
close	closed	closed
cry	cried	cried
play	played	played

irregular verbs

be	was	been
go	went	gone
have	had	had
make	made	made
swim	swam	swum
break	broke	broken

Ü 20.1. What have they done today?

Write down what they have done in your exercise book.

Example: Mike and Linda have gone out.

Ü 20.2. Irregular verb jets

Complete the planes and write the forms of the verbs in the chart in your exercise book.

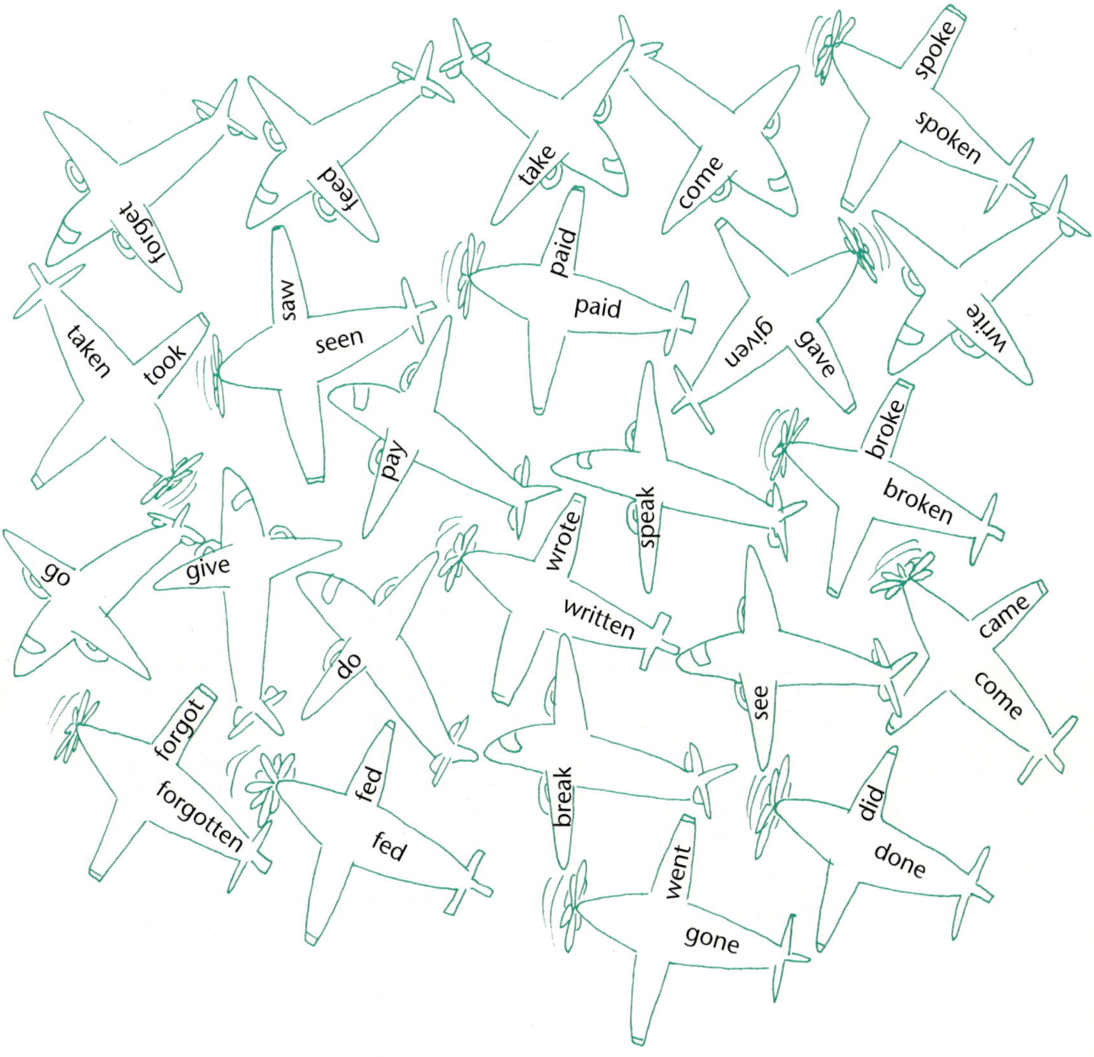

infinitive	past	past participle
take	took	taken
forget		

Ü 20.3. My day

Over to you. In the evening your mother wants to know what you have done during the day. Match the activities to the phrases and write sentences in your exercise book.

brush my teeth – take the dog for a walk – have lunch – clean my bike – watch TV – take photos – wash – play football – have breakfast – play with my friend – relax – go to school – ride my bike – drink … – have dinner

Example: I've = I have brushed my teeth.

How to use the present perfect / 1

Es gibt 3 eindeutig zu beschreibende Situationen, in denen das *present perfect* benutzt werden muss.

Erstens dann, wenn du eine Verbindung zwischen Vergangenheit und Gegenwart ausdrücken willst. Normalerweise sind Vergangenheit und Gegenwart zwei verschiedene Kreise, die sich nicht berühren.

Wenn du zeigen willst, dass etwas sowohl zur Vergangenheit als auch zur Gegenwart gehört – z. B. wenn du über Erfahrungen sprichst, die du in der Vergangenheit gemacht hast und die bis heute andauern oder die sich inzwischen geändert haben, dann musst du das *present perfect* benutzen.

Folgende *signal words* zeigen dir, dass du das *present perfect* benutzen musst:

up to now – ever – never – so far – not yet

Ü 20.4. Have you ever?

Look at the pictures. Form sentences with the present perfect and write them in your exercise book.

No, never. – Yes, I have. – Yes, of course. – No, that's impossible. – What are you thinking about? – Yes, I'm sure.

Example: Have you ever seen an elephant with two heads? No, never.

How to use the present perfect / 2

Zum Zweiten musst du das *present perfect* verwenden, wenn sich eine Handlung unmittelbar vor der Gegenwart ereignet hat und soeben beendet worden ist.

The plane has just landed.
Das Flugzeug ist gerade eben gelandet. Nun ist es da.

The teacher has left the classroom.
Vor einem winzigen Augenblick hat der Lehrer das Klassenzimmer verlassen.

Ü 20.5. A houseman

to attend – teilnehmen

Mother is attending an important conference in London. Our father is doing the housework. Later he tells his wife on the phone what he has done.
Write down what he is doing and what he has done.

	present progressive form		**present perfect**
make	He is making breakfast.		He has made breakfast.
do the washing-up	______		______
dry	______		______
water	______		______
make	______		______
wash	______	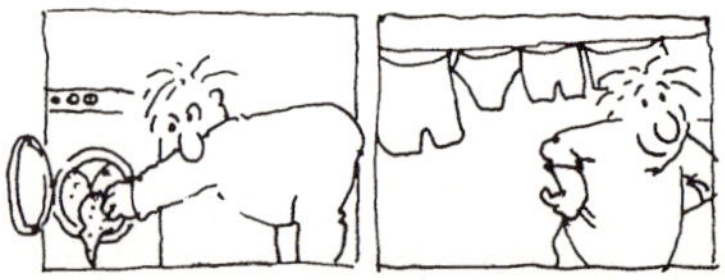	______

______________  ______________ clean

______________  ______________ cook

______________  ______________ lay

Ü 20.6. Peggy goes on holiday

Peggy's mother is waiting downstairs in the hall. She is waiting for Peggy. They are late. Look at the pictures and complete the dialogue. Afterwards write it down in your exercise book.

I haven't ... yet

Peggy's mother	**Peggy**
Come on, then.	(finish / hair) I haven't finished my hair yet.
I'm in a hurry.	(clean / shoes)
I can't wait any longer.	(brush / teeth)
The train leaves at 7.30.	(find / warm sweater)
It's already 7.15.	(telephone Anne)
You're always late.	(pack / suitcase)
You haven't packed your suitcase yet! Well then, let's stay at home.	

How to use the present perfect / 3

Drittens musst du im Englischen das *present perfect* verwenden, wenn ein Vorgang bereits in der Vergangenheit begonnen hat, in der Gegenwart aber noch andauert. Im Deutschen lässt sich oft ein „jetzt schon“ ergänzen.

Die wichtigsten Signalwörter sind *since* und *for*. Kommen diese Wörter in einem Satz vor, dann ist es sicher nicht falsch, das *present perfect* oder sogar das *present perfect continuous* zu verwenden.

Since hat etwas mit einem Zeitpunkt zu tun.

For verwendest du im Zusammenhang mit einem Zeitraum, wobei es unterschiedliche Bedeutung haben kann: *for three days* kann nicht nur „seit drei Tagen“ heißen, sondern auch „3 Tage lang“.

Beispiel: *It rained for three days when we were in Rom.*
Es regnete drei Tage lang, als wir in Rom waren.

Dieser Vorgang ist abgeschlossen und steht daher im *simple past.*

since	*for*
since + Zeitpunkt sagt aus, wann ein Zustand oder Vorgang angefangen hat *It has been raining since Monday.* = Zeitpunkt, an dem es anfing zu regnen	*for* + Zeitraum sagt aus, wie lange der Zustand oder Vorgang bereits andauert *It has been raining for three days.* = Zeitraum, über den sich der Regen bereits erstreckt

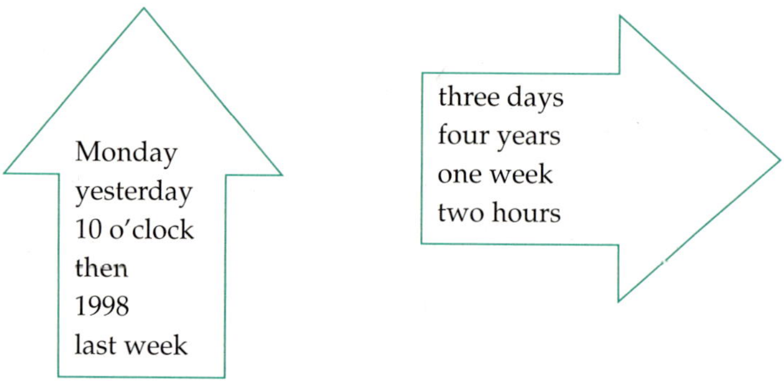

Ü 20.7. *since* or *for*

Put the phrases into the right boxes.

since	**for**
last week	

last week – two hours – 1990 – Monday – a few seconds – two years – five minutes – 1st May – Easter – our first meeting – one o’clock – a long time

Ü 20.8. Practise the present perfect / present perfect continuous

Fill in the gaps.

1. We are now living in Kiel where we _______________ (live) for almost seven years.
2. Our grandfather _______________ (be) in hospital since July.
3. Aunt Judy _______________ (live) in that house for many years.
4. I _______________ (not see) Peter since last Christmas.
5. My car is a Volkswagen. I _______________ (have) it for three years.
6. Catherine works in a bank. She _______________ (be) in a bank for five years.
7. Alan has a headache. He _______________ (have) a headache since he got up this morning.
8. I'm learning English. I _______________ (learn) English for quite a long time.

Ü 20.9. Decide: *for* or *since*

Complete the sentences.

1. Jill has been in Ireland ____since____ Monday.
2. Jill has been in Ireland ____________ three days.
3. My aunt has lived in Australia ____________ 15 years.
4. Margaret is in her office. She has been there ____________ 7 o'clock.
5. Sarah is an old friend. I have known her ____________ a long time.
6. The bus is late. We've been waiting ____________ 20 minutes.
7. Nobody lives in those houses. They have been empty ____________ many years.
8. Mark has been ill ____________ a long time. He has been in hospital ____________ October.

Ü 20.10. Final test

Fill in the present perfect forms of the verbs.

1. After he ______________ (write) his letter, he is going for a walk.
2. They ______________ (not clean) the house from top to bottom yet.
3. I hope that they ______________ (clean) the house at last and that Tommy ______________ (do) his homework.
4. We ______________ already ______________ (show) them pictures.
5. ______________ you ______________ (eat) the pudding yet?
6. I ______________ (see) the film "Titanic" three times.
7. I ______________ (never / see) any of Arnold Schwarzenegger's films.
8. But I ______________ (always / want) to see one.
9. How much of our homework ______________ you ______________ (do) you since I went away?
10. Mr. Black ______________ (fly) to London four times since August.
11. He ______________ (arrive) at the station.
12. My parents ______________ (have) their car for two months now.
13. ______________ you ______________ (ever / see) a tiger riding an elephant?
14. Look at those fantastic shoes. I ______________ (already / buy) a pair.
15. Peggy ______________ (not write) to her girlfriend Sue for three weeks.
16. Our football team ______________ (not lose) a match since the season began.
17. I ______________ (already / have) a CD player for two years.
18. Sorry, Jim. I ______________ (not finish) this letter yet.

21. Future

Übungsziel:
Die Formen der Zukunft kennen lernen und sie benutzen können

Um zu beschreiben, dass sich ein Ereignis in der Zukunft abspielen wird, hast du im Englischen zwei Möglichkeiten.

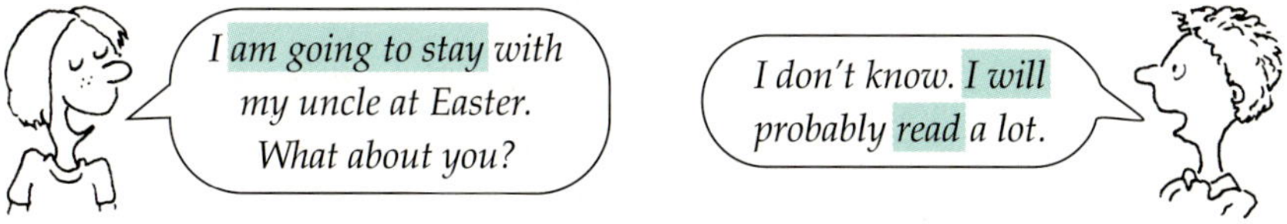

going to	*will*
fest geplante Zukunft	wahrscheinlich eintretende Zukunft

Das Futur mit *going to* verwendest du, wenn du eine schon vorher gefasste Absicht oder einen schon vorher geplanten Ablauf ausdrücken willst.

Das Futur mit *will* verwendest du gewöhnlich, um Vorhersagen zu machen über Ereignisse, die wahrscheinlich eintreten.

Du kannst im Englischen selten wie im Deutschen einfach das Präsens verwenden, um etwas Zukünftiges zu beschreiben.

Es gibt jedoch Ausnahmen – nämlich fest vereinbarte Termine: *Our office opens again next Monday.*

The future with *going to*

Singular	1st	*I am*	*going to*	Verb im Infinitiv	…
	2nd	*You are*			
	3rd	*He is* / *She is* / *It is*			
Plural	1st	*We are*			
	2nd	*You are*			
	3rd	*They are*			

Meist werden die abgekürzten Formen verwendet:
I'm going to do, you're going to do, he's / she's / it's going to do, we're going to do, you're going to do, they're going to do.

Das Futur mit *going to* wird immer mit einer Form von *to be* und *going to* gebildet. Danach folgt immer das Verb im Infinitiv.

Ü 21.1. What are the people going to do?

Write sentences in your exercise book.

Example: Chris is going to lie in the sun.

Ü 21.2. Over to you

What are you going to do next weekend?

1. I'm going to get up at ________________.
2. I'm going to have breakfast at ________________.
3. I'm going to leave home at ________________.
4. I'm going to have lunch with ________________.
5. I'm going to meet my friends at ________________.
6. I'm going to have supper at ________________.
7. I'm going to go out to ________________.
8. I'm going to return at ________________.
9. I'm going to be in bed at ________________.

Ü 21.3. A birthday invitation

Rewrite the letter using the given words and phrases.

____

________________,

It's ________________ next ________________ and I'm going to ________________.

Can you come? ________________! We'll have ________________ and ________________,

lots of ________________ and lots of ________________. The ________________ starts

at ________________. ________________ Saturday!

____

____

Joanne – Lots of love – I hope so – food – York, 30-11-1998 – have a party – party – fun – Dear Pat – games – prizes – four o'clock – my birthday – See you on – Saturday

Ü 21.4. On the telephone

Pete's phoning Ian to invite him to his birthday party next week. Can you put the sentences into the right order? Then rewrite the dialogue in your exercise book.

Pete: Thanks, Mr. Greenwood. … Hello? Ian? 6
Pete: I'm glad you can come. Bye. 18
Mr. Greenwood: Yes, speaking. 3
Pete: Oh, the usual sort of party food – sausages, cold chicken, salad, bread … and there'll be cider and shandy, and my Dad's going to make some fruit punch.
Ian: Yes, seven o'clock is perfect. How many people are going to be there?
Ian: I'd love to come. Which day?
Mr. Greenwood: Hello … Chippenham 4679.
Ian: Hi, Pete, what do you want?
Pete: This is Pete Steelforth, Ian's friend. Is Ian there, please?
Ian: Yes fine. What time on Saturday?
Pete: Well, I'm going to ask about twenty-five people – and I suppose about twenty will come.
Ian: It sounds delicious. Thanks for asking me. I'm really looking forward to it.
Mr. Greenwood: Just a minute, Pete, I'll see if he's here. Hello? Pete? He's coming to the phone now.
Pete: Hello, is that Mr. Greenwood?
Pete: I'm going to have a birthday party next weekend. Can you come?
Pete: Mum says, Saturday is the best day. I'll be fourteen on Thursday but I'm going to have the party at the weekend.
Ian: What are we going to eat?
Pete: About seven o'clock. Is that all right?

The future with *will*

Do you know this little song? It used to be very popular.

When I was just a little girl,
I asked my mother what will be.
Will I be pretty, will I be rich?
That's what my mother said:

Que serà, serà,
Whatever will be, will be
The future's not our's to see
Que serà, serà.

Wenn du ausdrücken willst, was wahrscheinlich in der Zukunft passieren wird, dann kannst du das Futur mit *will* verwenden.

Singular		**short forms**		**long forms**	
	1st	*I'll read*	*the newspaper*	*I will read*	*the newspaper*
	2nd	*You'll read*	*the newspaper*	*You will read*	*the newspaper*
	3rd	*He'll read*	*the newspaper*	*He will read*	*the newspaper*
	3rd	*She'll read*	*the newspaper*	*She will read*	*the newspaper*
	3rd	*It'll read*	*the newspaper*	*It will read*	*the newspaper*

Plural					
	1st	*We'll read*	*the newspaper*	*We will read*	*the newspaper*
	2nd	*You'll read*	*the newspaper*	*You will read*	*the newspaper*
	3rd	*They'll read*	*the newspaper*	*They will read*	*the newspaper*

Das Futur mit *will* wird aus *will* und dem Infinitiv eines Verbs gebildet. *Will* ist in allen Personen gleich.
Häufig wird statt *will* die Kurzform *'ll* verwendet.
Die Kurzform der Verneinung *will not* ist *won't*.

Ü 21.5. Birthday party

Here are some boys and girls who are all thinking of Fred's party next weekend. What will they do, if they go to the party?

Example: Mark will take some cassettes.

Ü 21.6. My dream island

This is what some pupils said about their dream island. Just read the descriptions.

Pat: My island will always be quiet and sunny. The water will be very blue and I'll catch fish every day. Every month a special plane will arrive with extra food and other things I'll need. No one will be allowed to visit my island without my permission.

permission – Erlaubnis

Mark: I'll make my own bread and I'll pick fresh fruit. Nobody will be there to tell me when to go to bed. Every day I'll make a mark on a tree to measure how many days I've been on the island. The sun will shine for fifteen hours a day and I'll make friends with the natives on the island. I'll drink milk from coconuts.

natives – hier: Eingeborene

Anna: I'll be alone on my island but I'll have a radio and I'll be able to hear what's happening in the rest of the world.

John: I'll go hunting, swimming and fishing. My house will be a little wooden cabin on a cliff. There'll be no pollution and no factories.

cabin – hier: Hütte
pollution – Umweltverschmutzung

Ü 21.7. Your dream island

Imagine that you're going to travel to an island when school finishes. What kind of island are you going to find? You can choose. Write down your answers.

1. Where will your island be?
2. What kind of plants will grow there?
3. Will there be any animals on the island? Are they safe or dangerous?
4. What will the weather be like? Will it be the same all the time?
5. Will there be any other people on the island?
6. Will the other people on the island be friendly or will they be enemies?
7. What will you eat?
8. You can take one CD with you. Which one will you take?
9. You can have one book. Which book do you want?
10. You can take one luxury item. What will you choose?

enemy – Feind

luxury item – Luxusgegenstand

Use phrases like these:

On my island I'll …
I won't …
There will be …
There won't be …

Ü 21.8. Your future

Now look into the future. Write about your own future.

Will I be rich?
Will I get married?
How many children will I have?
What will my hobbies be?
Where will I travel?
What will my problems be?
Will I be happy?
What sort of person will I marry?
What sort of job will I have?
What will I look like at 35?
What will I look like at 75?

22. The final Chapter

Your page

This is me! Fill in the missing words and draw some small pictures.

Hello! My name's ______________________________

I'm _______________ (your age). I'm ___________________________ (nationality). My birthday is in _______________________ (month).

My star sign is _________________________ (sign of the zodiac).

sign of the zodiac – Tierkreiszeichen

I live in a __________________ (flat / house). My father is ____________________________ (his job). My mother is ____________________________ (her job). My favourite colour is ___________.

I like _______________ and ____________________ (2 sports).

I like _______________ and ____________________ (2 hobbies).

What's my favourite thing? My ________________________ (favourite object / thing) of course! My favourite film is ______________________ (favourite film). I like reading _______________________ (funny books / educational books / mystery stories / animal stories / detective stories).

I play the _________________________ (musical instrument). I have a pet _______________ (dog / cat / horse / bird / rabbit / hamster / fish).

My favourite food is _______________. My favourite popsinger is ____________________________. My favourite subject in school is ____________________. When I leave school I want to be ____________________ (your job). My best friends in class are called ____ (names of your friends). My favourite person in my class is _________________________

That's great! You reached the end!
You have worked hard and now you are able to say a lot of things in English.
Think about what you have done.
When did you start learning English?
How long have you been learning English?
You have learnt to say a lot of things. Try to find out what you can say in English.
Here is a list. Mark all the things in the bubbles that you can say.
I'm sure you can find more things to say in English.

I can
- give information about myself
- introduce my friends and myself
- talk about my hobbies
- talk about things I like or dislike
- give reasons for my likes and dislikes
- talk about friends
- talk about my family

I can
- ask for something to eat or to drink
- offer something to eat or to drink
- buy the things I need
- phone my family and my friends
- describe what people are doing at the moment

I can
-

I can
- talk about yesterday's and today's weather
- say what one can see in London
- ask how to get to important buildings
- read recipes
- interview people about their job or the job they'd like to have
- write reports about an interview
- write reports about past events

Write in your exercise book if there is not enough space. Try to practise your English. Think about what you have to say.
Good luck!

Irregular verbs

infinitive	simple past	past participle	
be [iː]	was / were	been [iː]	sein
become [ʌ]	became [eɪ]	become [ʌ]	werden
begin [ɪ]	began [æ]	begun [ʌ]	beginnen
bet [e]	bet [e]	bet [e]	wetten
bite [aɪ]	bit [ɪ]	bitten [ɪ]	beißen
blow [əʊ]	blew [uː]	blown [əʊ]	blasen, wehen
break [eɪ]	broke [əʊ]	broken [əʊ]	(zer)brechen
bring [ɪ]	brought [ɔː]	brought [ɔː]	bringen, mitbringen
build [ɪ]	built [ɪ]	built [ɪ]	bauen
buy [aɪ]	bought [ɔː]	bought [ɔː]	kaufen
catch [æ]	caught [ɔː]	caught [ɔː]	fangen
choose [uː]	chose [əʊ]	chosen [əʊ]	(aus)wählen
come [ʌ]	came [eɪ]	come [ʌ]	kommen
cost [ɒ]	cost [ɒ]	cost [ɒ]	kosten
cut [ʌ]	cut [ʌ]	cut [ʌ]	schneiden
do [uː]	did [ɪ]	done [ʌ]	tun, machen
draw [ɔː]	drew [uː]	drawn [ɔː]	zeichnen
drink [ɪ]	drank [æ]	drunk [ʌ]	trinken
drive [aɪ]	drove [əʊ]	driven [ɪ]	fahren
eat [iː]	ate [e]	eaten [iː]	essen
fall [ɔː]	fell [e]	fallen [ɔː]	fallen
feed [iː]	fed [e]	fed [e]	füttern
feel [iː]	felt [e]	felt [e]	fühlen
find [aɪ]	found [aʊ]	found [aʊ]	finden
fly [aɪ]	flew [uː]	flown [əʊ]	fliegen
forget [e]	forgot [ɒ]	forgotten [ɒ]	vergessen
get [e]	got [ɒ]	got [ɒ]	bekommen, werden
give [ɪ]	gave [eɪ]	given [ɪ]	geben
go [əʊ]	went [e]	gone [ɒ]	gehen
grow [əʊ]	grew [uː]	grown [əʊ]	wachsen, anbauen
have [æ]	had [æ]	had [æ]	haben
hear [ɪə]	heard [ɜː]	heard [ɜː]	hören
hide [aɪ]	hid [ɪ]	hidden [ɪ]	verstecken
hit [ɪ]	hit [ɪ]	hit [ɪ]	schlagen, treffen
hold [əʊ]	held [e]	held [e]	halten
hurt [ɜː]	hurt [ɜː]	hurt [ɜː]	verletzen
keep [iː]	kept [e]	kept [e]	(be)halten
know [əʊ]	knew [juː]	known [əʊ]	wissen, kennen
lay [eɪ]	laid [eɪ]	laid [eɪ]	legen
learn [ɜː]	learnt, learned [ɜː]	learnt, learned [ɜː]	lernen

infinitive	simple past	past participle	
leave [iː]	left [e]	left [e]	lassen, verlassen
lend [e]	lent [e]	lent [e]	leihen
lie [aɪ]	lay [eɪ]	lain [eɪ]	liegen
let [e]	let [e]	let [e]	lassen
lose [uː]	lost [ɒ]	lost [ɒ]	verlieren
make [eɪ]	made [eɪ]	made [eɪ]	machen
mean [iː]	meant [e]	meant [e]	meinen, bedeuten
meet [iː]	met [e]	met [e]	treffen
pay [eɪ]	paid [eɪ]	paid [eɪ]	(be)zahlen
put [ʊ]	put [ʊ]	put [ʊ]	setzen, stellen, legen
read [iː]	read [e]	read [e]	lesen
ride [aɪ]	rode [əʊ]	ridden [ɪ]	reiten, fahren
ring [ɪ]	rang [æ]	rung [ʌ]	klingeln
run [ʌ]	ran [æ]	run [ʌ]	rennen, laufen
say [eɪ]	said [e]	said [e]	sagen, sprechen
see [iː]	saw [ɔː]	seen [iː]	sehen
sell [e]	sold [əʊ]	sold [əʊ]	verkaufen
send [e]	sent [e]	sent [e]	schicken
set [e]	set [e]	set [e]	setzen, legen
shake [eɪ]	shook [ʊ]	shaken [eɪ]	schütteln
show [əʊ]	showed [əʊ]	shown [əʊ]	zeigen
shut [ʌ]	shut [ʌ]	shut [ʌ]	schließen
shrink [ɪ]	shrank [æ]	shrunk [ʌ]	eingehen
sing [ɪ]	sang [æ]	sung [ʌ]	singen
sit [ɪ]	sat [æ]	sat [æ]	sitzen
sleep [iː]	slept [e]	slept [e]	schlafen
speak [iː]	spoke [əʊ]	spoken [əʊ]	sprechen
spell [e]	spelt [e]	spelt [e]	buchstabieren, rechtschreiben
spend [e]	spent [e]	spent [e]	ausgeben
stand [æ]	stood [ʊ]	stood [ʊ]	stehen
steal [iː]	stole [əʊ]	stolen [əʊ]	stehlen
swim [ɪ]	swam [æ]	swum [ʌ]	schwimmen
take [eɪ]	took [ʊ]	taken [eɪ]	nehmen
teach [iː]	taught [ɔː]	taught [ɔː]	unterrichten
tell [e]	told [əʊ]	told [əʊ]	erzählen, sagen
think [ɪ]	thought [ɔː]	thought [ɔː]	denken
throw [əʊ]	threw [uː]	thrown [əʊ]	werfen
understand [æ]	understood [ʊ]	understood [ʊ]	verstehen
wake [eɪ]	woke [əʊ]	woken [əʊ]	aufwachen, wecken
wear [eə]	wore [ɔː]	worn [ɔː]	tragen (Kleidung)
win [ɪ]	won [ʌ]	won [ʌ]	gewinnen
write [aɪ]	wrote [əʊ]	written [ɪ]	schreiben

Die Lerntipps im ersten Band von „Grammatik und Wortschatz“ (mentor Lernhilfe Band 540) haben sich mit dem Vokabellernen beschäftigt.

Hier geht es nun um Hausaufgaben und Klassenarbeiten.

Wie oft stellst du dir durchschnittlich ein Bein?

Eine blöde Frage, nicht wahr?

Wörtlich genommen stellt man sich ja wirklich nur selten ein Bein. Aber im übertragenen Sinne tun viele es ziemlich oft.

Viele Menschen (nicht nur Schüler!) haben eine auffällige Verwandtschaft zu Faultieren. „Was du heute kannst besorgen, das verschieb getrost auf morgen!", lautet ihr Motto. Oder: „Hausaufgaben sind Luxus, und Luxus kann ich mir nicht leisten."

Womit wir schon beim leidigen Thema wären: den Hausaufgaben. Sicher, Arbeit hat immer mit Anstrengung zu tun, und die versucht man gerne zu vermeiden. Aber bezogen auf Hausaufgaben gilt leider der Satz: Der Preis für einen kurzen Lustgewinn ist oft lange Unlust.

Wer Hausaufgaben nicht oder nur schlampig macht, stellt sich wirklich selbst ein Bein – leider fällt er oft erst einige Zeit später auf die Nase und bemerkt den Zusammenhang zur früheren Nachlässigkeit nicht. Hausaufgaben vernünftig zu machen, erspart dir auf Dauer Nachteile in Form schlechterer Noten und eines größeren Zeitaufwands.
Vielleicht überzeugen dich (bzw. deinen „inneren Schweinehund") die folgenden fünf Argumente:

- **Argument 1:**
  Wer Hausaufgaben schlampig und „schnell-schnell" erledigt, lernt nichts dazu. Schreibt der Lehrer überraschend in der nächsten Stunde eine Arbeit oder fragt er dich ab, stehst du dumm da.

- **Argument 2:**
  Hausaufgaben sind Übungsgelegenheiten. Wer jetzt nichts lernt, muss es irgendwann einmal nachholen, spätestens vor der nächsten angesagten Prüfung.

  Der kurzfristige Zeitgewinn ist also nur Schein!

- **Argument 3:**
  Schlimmer noch: Wer bei den Hausaufgaben schlampt, muss den Stoff später praktisch neu lernen und das kostet viel mehr Zeit, ist sehr aufwendig und erzeugt bzw. verstärkt Prüfungsangst.

  Oft hat man außerdem niemanden zur Hand, der einem den Stoff dann erklären kann.

- **Argument 4:**
  Langfristig wird die Zeit länger, die man für das Anfertigen einer Hausaufgabe braucht, denn man muss all das, was man früher nicht richtig gelernt hat, nachschauen und nacharbeiten.

- **Argument 5:**
  Wenn man neuen Stoff lernen will/muss, aber den alten, der die Basis bildet, nicht begriffen bzw. eingeübt hat, ist das, als wollte man eine Jacke in der Luft aufhängen - sie fällt herunter. Der alte Stoff ist sozusagen der Haken, an den man den neuen hängen kann.

Fazit:

Wer bei Hausaufgaben schlampt, spart nur im Moment Zeit - auf Dauer muss er sie dann doch aufwenden, meist sogar noch mehr! Wer hingegen clever ist, macht seine Hausaufgaben regelmäßig – dann braucht er weit weniger Zeit bei der Prüfungsvorbereitung und bei späteren Hausaufgaben und hat zugleich bessere Noten.

Und wenn du nun deine Hausaufgaben sinnvoll machst, ist auch ein anderes nerviges Thema leichter zu erledigen:

Klassenarbeiten vorbereiten clever und mit System

Die Vorbereitung beginnt viel früher, als viele meinen: nämlich in jeder laufenden Unterrichtsstunde, die zur nächsten Arbeit gehört, sowie bei den täglichen Hausaufgaben. Du kannst dir viel Zeit und Nerven unmittelbar vor der Arbeit sparen, wenn du das wirklich ernst nimmst. Denn das hatten wir ja grade schon: Was du im Laufe der Zeit nicht lernst, musst du irgendwann einmal nachholen. Und das ist meist viel anstrengender!

Fünf Schritte umfasst eine sinnvolle, langfristig angelegte und damit clevere Vorbereitung:

1. Schritt:
aktive Teilnahme am Unterricht

2. Schritt:
ordentliche, übersichtliche und fehlerfreie Heftführung

3. Schritt:
sorgfältiges Erledigen der Hausaufgaben und Nachbereitung der Unterrichtsstunde (Nachbereitung bedeutet, dass du dich nochmals kurz mit dem beschäftigst, was du in der Unterrichtsstunde gelernt hast, und Unverstandenes sofort zu klären versuchst.)

4. Schritt:
laufende Wiederholung

5. Schritt:
Vorbereitung unmittelbar vor der Klassenarbeit

Jeder dieser Schritte ist wie eine Stufe auf dem Weg zu einer erfolgreich bewältigten Klassenarbeit. Wenn du eine Stufe auslässt, werden die späteren Stufen umso höher.

Solltest du z.B. deine Hefte schlampig führen, wirst du schon von Stunde zu Stunde nicht gründlich lernen können und bald kennst du dich dann in deinem Heft gar nicht mehr aus.

Oder du lernst sogar falsche Dinge: Es ist doch z.B. wirklich unangenehm, in einer Klassenarbeit Vokabeln bloß deshalb falsch zu schreiben, weil man sie falsch aus dem eigenen Heft gelernt hat!

Falls du sogar erst unmittelbar vor der Arbeit anfängst richtig zu lernen, ist der Arbeitsberg oft so hoch, dass du ihn nur unter gewaltigen Anstrengungen erklimmen kannst und trotzdem oft wenig erfolgreich abschneiden wirst.

Und dass es ein bisschen länger dauert, Vokabeln vernünftig zu lernen, weißt du ja schon.

Am letzten Tag vor der Arbeit kannst du nicht mehr so viele neue Vokabeln in dich „reinstopfen" – da besteht die Gefahr, dass du vieles durcheinander bringst, dich gar nicht mehr erinnerst oder sonstige Fehler machst.

Auf die Vorbereitung unmittelbar vor der Arbeit kann man freilich nicht ganz verzichten, denn man muss den Stoff ja auffrischen. Die Zeit, die du dafür benötigst, wird aber umso kürzer, je mehr du die Schritte 1 bis 4 beachtet hast. Denn du brauchst den Stoff eben nur zu wiederholen, nicht praktisch neu zu lernen. Außerdem gibt es keine tieferen Verständnisprobleme mehr, die in der knappen Zeit oft nicht mehr klärbar sind.

Und so kannst du die Vorbereitung unmittelbar vor einer Klassenarbeit clever und mit System betreiben:

- **Überblick:**
  Spätestens 10 Tage vor der Arbeit solltest du wissen, welche Stoffgebiete genau drankommen. Frag ruhig deinen Lehrer/deine Lehrerin, wenn er/sie es nicht von sich aus rechtzeitig mitteilt.

  Und frag ruhig nach, wenn die Antwort sehr allgemein ist (zum Beispiel „Stoff ist alles, was wir gemacht haben")!

- **Aufteilung des Stoffes:**
  Teile dir den zu wiederholenden Stoff (und die Vokabeln) in kleine, verdaubare Portionen auf!

Wie viel Zeit du pro Tag brauchst, hängt natürlich davon ab, ob du den Stoff nur wiederholen oder praktisch neu lernen musst.

Nun erstellst du einen Arbeitsplan. Und immer wenn du einen Abschnitt geschafft hast, kannst du genussvoll einen Punkt deines Arbeitsplanes durchstreichen. So siehst du, wie der Berg immer kleiner wird - das ist wichtig fürs Selbstbewusstsein.

Wenn du eine Portion bearbeitest, solltest du übrigens zunächst immer erst den entsprechenden Hefteintrag studieren, bevor du dich an die Arbeit machst.

- **Aufteilung des Vorbereitungszeitraums:**
Der erste Abschnitt dient dazu, dass du den Stoff einmal gründlich durcharbeitest bzw. wiederholst. Drei bis vier Tage vor der Arbeit solltest du alles kapiert und die Vokabeln gelernt haben. Dann kommt garantiert kein Stress auf!
Im zweiten Abschnitt übst du gezielt Dinge, die drankommen. So gewöhnst du dich an die Aufgabenstellung und weißt besser, was von dir erwartet wird. Außerdem kannst du jetzt noch das eine oder andere Problem lösen.

- **Training auf Zeit betreiben:**
In der Klassenarbeit muss man ja eine Aufgabe nicht nur überhaupt beantworten können, sondern es in einer gewissen Zeit schaffen. Viele machen den Fehler, das nicht schon vor der Prüfung zu trainieren, und ärgern sich dann, wenn sie die Arbeit verhauen.

Lasse dir von deinem Lehrer/deiner Lehrerin sagen, wie viel Zeit du für die Beantwortung einer Aufgabe brauchen darfst, und übe das dann während der Vorbereitung.

Wenn möglich, sollte man das Zeittraining schon bei den laufenden Hausaufgaben durchziehen (natürlich erst dann, wenn man den Stoff kapiert hat).

- **Der letzte Tag:**
Lerne am letzten Tag nichts mehr, was dich noch verwirren könnte, sondern beschränke dich auf eine großzügige Wiederholung.

Vor allem jedoch solltest du am letzten Tag das tun, was dir Spaß macht und womit du dich entspannen kannst.

Wer am letzten Tag noch ein schwieriges Kapitel lernen muss, das er ständig vor sich hergeschoben hat, darf sich nicht wundern, wenn er Angst bekommt und unsicher wird. Zudem findet man jetzt oft niemanden mehr, der einem helfen kann.

Wenn du dieses Programm durchgezogen hast, bist du toll vorbereitet und es sollte klappen in der Klassenarbeit!

Stichwortverzeichnis

f. bedeutet: Du findest das Stichwort auf der angegebenen und der folgenden Seite.
ff. bedeutet: Du findest das Stichwort auf der angegebenen und mehreren folgenden Seiten.

P

R

S

V

W

Z

mentor Lernhilfe

Englisch

5./6. Klasse

Grammatik und Wortschatz:
Grundlagen, Teil 2

Rainer Iwen

Lösungsteil

(an der Perforation heraustrennen)

Nach dem Heraustrennen bitte hier klammern

In Zusammenarbeit
mit Langenscheidt

mentor
Eine Klasse besser.

Übung 2.1. S. 8

skyscraper – hospital – library – stadium – factory – office – tower – post office – police station – Underground / Tube – railway station – subway – park – square – avenue – corner – traffic lights – bus stop – car park – bench – phone box – cinema – letterbox – litterbin – fountain – monument – street-lamp

Übung 2.2. S. 9

1. I'm going to the library.
2. I'm going to school.
3. I'm going to the castle.
4. I'm going to the post office.
5. I'm going to the stadium.
6. I'm going to the railway station.

Übung 2.3. S. 10

1. school
2. church
3. museum
4. cinema
5. post office
6. bank
7. supermarket
8. factory
9. police station
10. telephone box
11. public toilets
12. station
13. newsstand
14. car park
15. hotel
16. park

Übung 2.5. S. 11

2. library
3. hospital
4. hotel
5. stadium
6. post office
7. school
8. factory
9. railway station
10. police station

Übung 2.6. S. 11

Write a description like this:
Where I live there are few parks and many large buildings. There is an old castle and some playgrounds. There are expensive supermarkets and modern department stores …

Übung 3.1. S. 12 / 13

bus – car – ambulance – motorbike – van – bicycle – caravan – helicopter – aeroplane – tricycle – train – tram – lorry – fire-engine – tractor

1. lorry – 2. bus – 3. car – 4. bicycle – 5. taxi – 6. fire-engine – 7. aeroplane – 8. tram – 9. tricycle – 10. motorbike – 11. train – 12. van – 13. caravan – 14. tractor – 15. helicopter

Übung 3.2. S. 13

There are 3 bicycles. There are 2 lorries. There are 2 buses. There are 8 cars.

Übung 3.3. S. 14

Brenda is going to school by bus.
Ricky is going to his girl friend on foot.
Susan is going to the beach by car.
David is going to the post office by tram.

Übung 3.4. S. 15 / 16

The right order of the pictures:
4 / 3 / 6 / 2 / 5 / 1 / 7 / 8

1. It was Ricky's fault because the lady had the right of way.
2. Ricky didn't pay attention.

P: Did you see the accident? Y: Yes, I was there, when it happened.
P: Where did the accident happen? Y: It happened right here in Oxford Street.
P: When exactly did it happen? Y: It happened at 9.15 in the morning.
P: Was anyone hurt? Y: Yes, an old lady was hurt.

Übung 3.5.
S. 16

P: Who called the ambulance? Y: The boy who caused the accident called the ambulance.
P: When did the ambulance arrive? Y: The ambulance arrived 5 minutes later.
P: Whose fault was the accident? Y: I think, it was the fault of the boy. The lady had the right of way but the boy didn't pay attention.
P: Are you from Germany? Y: Yes, I am.
P: What's your name? Y: My name is …
P: Where in Germany do you live? Y: I'm from …
P: Are you on holiday here? Y: Yes, I am.

Übung 4.1.
S. 17

It was necessary to **read all** the instructions:

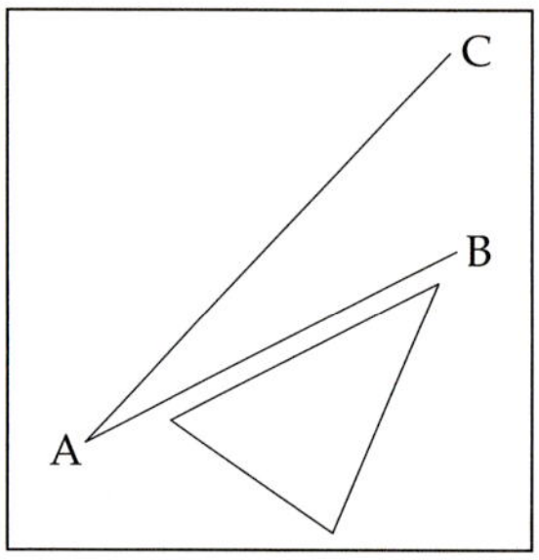

Übung 4.2.
S. 17

1F – 2J – 3G – 4B – 5H – 6I – 7C – 8E – 9A – 10D

Übung 4.3.
S. 18

1. Jump up and down.
2. Lift your arms.
3. Touch your head.
4. Put your left arm over your head.
5. Lift your left arm and lift your right arm.
6. Lie down and lift your feet.
7. Bend your arms.
8. Bend up and down.
9. Sit down.
10. Lift your left foot.
11. Lift your right foot.
12. Jump up and down and touch your head.
13. Jump up and down.
14. Touch your nose with your foot.
15. Stand on your head.

Übung 4.4.
S. 19

Don't cut up the magazine.
Don't open the fridge door.
Don't throw your teddy bear out of the window.
Don't climb on the table.
Don't write on your books.
Don't cross the road in front of a car.

Übung 4.5.
S. 20

Write sentences like this:
Don't play football with the bottle.
Don't draw on the board.
Don't write on the window-pane.
Don't do your homework here and now.
Don't stand on the desks.
Don't look out of the windows.

Übung 4.6. S. 20

Fasten seat belts – on a plane
Don't feed the animals – in a zoo
Be quiet please – in a library
Do not lean out of the window – in a train
Do not bring animals with you – in a restaurant
Queue this side – at a bus stop
Push / Pull – on a door
Bring your friends – in a shop
Don't smoke – at a petrol station

Übung 4.7. S. 21

2. Let's go to the zoo.
3. Let's watch the ship.
4. Let's drink (make) tea.
5. Let's take the dog for a walk.
6. Let's visit the art gallery.
7. Let's read a book.
8. Let's listen to the bird.

Übung 5.1. S. 23

1B / 2F / 3J / 4E / 5H / 6G / 7A / 8K / 9C / 10D / 11I

Übung 5.2. S. 24

Fred is in Central Park right in front of the biggest pond.

Übung 5.3. S. 25

1. Go straight on past the shoe shop till you come to the phone box.
2. Turn right at the phone box.
3. Go straight on past the supermarket on your left.
4. Cross the road at the cinema.
5. Then turn left at the next crossing.
6. The bank is on your right on the other side of the street.

Übung 5.4. S. 26

A: Excuse me, can you tell me the way to the station, please?
B: Yes, of course. Go straight on till you come to the end of the street. Then turn left.
A: Straight on till the end of the street and then to the left, is that right?
B: Yes, that's right. Walk straight on as far as the post office. Then take the first road on the left and the second on the right.
A: Can you tell me how far it is?
B: It's about half an hour from here.
A: Oh, that's a long way. Is there a bus to the station?
B: Yes, there is. The bus stop is right there on the other side of the street.
A: Thank you very much.
B: You're welcome. Goodbye.
A: Goodbye.

Übung 6.1. S. 28

2. them 3. us 4. it 5. them 6. her 7. it 8. us 9. him 10. it

Übung 6.2. S. 29

her – them – him – her – it – them – us – you – him

Übung 6.3. S. 30

your – his – her – its – our – your – their

John, are you looking for your book?
He often plays with his ball.
She plays in her room.
That is an old car. Its windows are broken.
We need new curtains for all our windows.
Where have you put your socks?
They are playing with their dolls.

Übung 6.4. S. 31

My language is Spanish.
Our language is Polish.
His language is German, French or Italian.
Her language is English.
Your language is German.
Their language is Swedish.
My language is Dutch.
Your language is Portuguese.
Her language is German.
Her language is Greek.
Their language is French.
My language is English.
His language is Finnish.
Our language is Danish.
Our language is Italian.
His language is Turkish.
Her language is French or Flemish.

Übung 6.5. S. 32

my kitchen – our room – Their – our – her – your – his – our – their

Übung 6.6. S. 33

yourself – himself – herself – itself – ourselves – yourselves – themselves

Übung 6.7. S. 33

1. myself 2. ourselves 3. ourselves 4. herself 5. himself 6. itself

Übung 7.1. S. 34

happy – angry – sad – tired – ashamed – confused – proud – scared – bored – nervous

Übung 7.2. S. 35

Individuelle Lösung

Übung 7.3. S. 36

Individuelle Lösung

Übung 7.4. S. 37 / 38

1. b) son, father, grandfather
   c) baby, teenager, grown-up

2. a) Sunday, Tuesday, Wednesday
   b) breakfast, dinner, tea
   c) spring, summer, autumn

3. a) hut, house, skyscraper
   b) bird, horse, elephant
   c) matchbox car, taxi, bus

Übung 7.5. S. 39

one syllable: thin – fat – old – tall – nice – loud

two syllables, ending in **-y, -er, -le, -ow**:
easy – narrow – noble – happy – funny – simple – clever – crazy – noisy

two syllables (rest): tired – modern

three or more syllables:
uncomfortable – fascinating – terrible – beautiful – wonderful – intelligent

Übung 7.6. S. 40

cold – colder – the coldest
beautiful – more beautiful – the most beautiful
clever – cleverer – the cleverest
large – larger – the largest
simple – simpler – the simplest
modern – more modern – the most modern
intelligent – more intelligent – the most intelligent
narrow – narrower – the narrowest
useful – more useful – the most useful

Übung 7.7. S. 41

2. The jeans on the left are expensive. The jeans in the middle are more expensive. The jeans on the right are the most expensive.
3. The boy on the left is fast. The boy in the middle is faster. The boy on the right is the fastest.
4. The monkey is strong. The pony is stronger. The elephant is the strongest.
5. Diving is exciting. Free climbing is more exciting. Bungee jumping is most exciting.
6. The girl on the left is beautiful. The girl in the middle is more beautiful. The girl on the right is the most beautiful girl.

Übung 7.8. S. 41

sweetest – pretty – blue – fair – smallest – youngest – older – tallest – good – best looking – nicest – most intelligent – good – funniest – loud – fastest – interesting – most boring

Übung 7.9. S. 43

1. much – more 2. many – more – the most 3. smaller – smaller – the smallest
4. a) Mabel is good at English, but Helen is the best. b) Mabel is good at German, too. Peter is better but Helen is the best. c) Peter is bad at biology, but Helen is even worse and Mabel is the worst.

Übung 7.10. S. 45

1. Line C is the longest. Line B is not as long as line C.
2. Line B is longer than line A and line C. Line A is shorter than line C. Line B is the longest line.

2. No, the green square is narrower than the white square.
3. No, the grey square is longer.
4. No, it is wider. It is 1,5 cm wide.
5. No, it's only 0,5 cm wider.
6. The green square is narrower than the white square.
7. The pale green square is as wide as the grey square.
8. The grey and the pale green squares are 1 cm wider than the green square.
9. The grey square is longer than the striped square.
10. The striped square is the widest one.

Übung 7.11. S. 46

The activities are:
visiting friends / going to the cinema – going shopping / lying in the sun – going to the disco / listening to music – playing golf / playing tennis – windsurfing / swimming – jogging / cycling – playing the guitar / painting

nice – nicer – nicest / interesting – more interesting – the most interesting / expensive – more expensive – the most expensive / difficult – more difficult – the most difficult / good – better – the best / hard – harder – the hardest / easy – easier – the easiest

Übung 7.12. S. 47

budgie – budgie – nicer – canary – canary – more beautiful – budgie – rabbit – quietest – guinea-pig – noisier – rabbit – goldfish – goldfish – most interesting – goldfish – cat – more interesting – goldfish – cat – more beautiful – cats – cats – the stinkiest – dog – bigger – more intelligent – dog – monkey – monkeys – the most intelligent – monkeys – the loveliest and funniest

Übung 8.1. S. 49

1. –	2. +	3. –	4. –	5. –
6. +	7. –	8. –	9. +	10. –

7 + 8

Übung 8.2. S. 49

get up – seven o'clock – half past eight – bike – half – nine o'clock – assembly – half past nine – eleven o'clock – twenty minutes – ten to eleven – ten past eleven – Quarter to one – cafeteria – teachers – hamburgers – carrots – pears – bad weather – library – books – sun – football – ten to four – bike – TV – a quarter past nine – bed

Übung 8.3./8.4. 8.5. S. 50/51

Individuelle Lösung

Übung 8.6. S. 52

2. English	6. history	11. woodwork
3. geography	8. music	13. cookery / domestic science
4. mathematics	9. physical education (PE)	14. drama
5. art	10. biology	15. needlework

Übung 8.7./8.8. S. 53

Individuelle Lösung

Übung 8.9. S. 54/55

A time table

Time	Mon	Tues	Wed	Thurs	Fri
9.00	assembly	assembly	assembly	assembly	assembly
9.20	German	English	German	maths	music
10.00	P.E.	English	English	science	science
10.40	morning break	morning break	morning break	morning break	morning break
11.00	maths	maths	geography	science	maths
12.00	R.E.	P.E.	art	music	biology
12.40	dinner break	dinner break	dinner break	dinner break	dinner break
2.00	art	history	maths	religious education	history
2.40	music	biology	art	cookery, woodwork	cookery, woodwork
3.20	English	geography	needlework	swimming	German
4.00	P.E.	drama	biology	swimming	film club

Übung 9.1. S. 56–60

to dig – to lie – to clean – to drink – to wash – to wipe – to wake up – to work – to live – to stand up – to sleep – to brush – to sit down – to get up – to rest – to polish

to cut – to burn – to stop – to wait – to go – to come – to bring – to lend – to tear – to send – to get – to carry – to give – to give back – to break – to pick up

to drive – to hide – to shine – to hurt – to ride – to swim – to fight – to kick – to creep – to sink – to pass – to fly – to shoot – to climb – to rain – to lose – to find

to learn – to expect – to think – to taste – to understand – to know – to say – to draw – to point at – to see – to remember – to ask – to hear – to forget – to teach – to believe – to look – to call – to hope – to listen to

to use – to wear – to follow – to pay – to exchange – to meet – to help – to steal

Übung 9.2. S. 60

1N / 2E / 3O / 4H / 5I / 6Q / 7D / 8M / 9B / 10R / 11L / 12T / 13S / 14P / 15C / 16J / 17G / 18F / 19A / 20K

Übung 9.3. S. 61

to make: 1A / 2C / 3E / 4F / 5H / 6B / 7J / 8I / 9D / 10G

to do: 1H / 2G / 3F / 4D / 5B / 6I / 7J / 8E / 9C / 10A

Übung 9.4. S. 62

does – makes – does – does – makes – does – do – makes

Übung 9.5. S. 62

making – make – do – do – do – do – do

Übung 9.6. S. 62

I do: my homework – the washing-up – right – a test – my best – wrong – the room

I make: the beds – breakfast – a fire – coffee – a noise – a mistake – a telephone call

Übung 9.7. S. 63

Hier kommt es darauf an, inhaltlich sinnvolle Sätze zu bilden, z. B.:
1. Take a piece of soap to the bathroom and bring back some towels.
2. Take the cups to the kitchen and bring back the vacuum cleaner.
3. Take the tools to the cellar and bring back father's hammer.
4. Take the magazines to your room and bring back your schoolbag.
5. Take the parcels to the post office and bring back some postcards.
6. Take the papers to our neighbour and bring back some stamps.
7. Take the shirts to Betty's room and bring back Betty's sandals.
8. Take the black shoes to the shoemaker's and bring back some black shoe polish.

Übung 9.8. S. 63

1. listen to 2. hear 3. hear 4. listen – hear

Übung 9.9. S. 64

1. see 2. looking 3. watch 4. see – look

Übung 9.10. S. 64

1. hears – understand – saying
2. hears
3. look – watch
4. looks
5. looks
6. see
7. looks – sees – seen
8. looks
9. hear – listen

Übung 9.11. S. 64 / 65

1. get 2. become 3. get 4. become 5. get 6. became

Übung 9.12. **S. 65**
2. He gets off at Victoria Station.
3. He goes to a restaurant because he is very hungry.
4. He orders a beefsteak.
5. He shouts in a loud voice.
6. He shouts, "When shall I become a beefsteak?"
7. The waiter answers: "I hope never".
8. No you can't. You can get a beefsteak. You can become a waiter.

Übung 10.1. **S. 67**
Hier kommt es darauf an inhaltlich sinnvolle Sätze zu bilden, z. B.:
A dog can bark very loudly but it can't see well.
A budgie can sing very well but it can't smell very well.
A lion can climb trees but it can't sing.
A monkey can eat bananas but it can't bark.
A horse can pull cars but it can't catch mice.
A snake can live a long time without water but it can't jump.
A cat can catch mice but it can't see well.
A bear can swim but it can't sing.

Übung 10.2. **S. 68**
1. sail 2. ride a bike 3. dance 4. play tennis 5. swim 6. ride a horse 7. go skiing 8. climb a tree 9. skate 10. play football 11. go fishing 12. collect stamps

Übung 10.3. **S. 68**
Individuelle Lösung

Übung 10.4. **S. 69**
Can you help me?
I can't see very well.
Can you say that again, please.
I can't do it. It's too difficult.
Can you spell that word, please?
Can I open the window?
Can you show me your homework?
Can I write that word on the board?
Can you pronounce this word?

Übung 10.5. **S. 70**
Bilde sinnvolle Sätze. Auch andere Sätze sind möglich.
Fred couldn't climb trees with his broken arm but he could go to bed.
Fred couldn't use his computer but he could go out for a walk.
Fred couldn't play the guitar but he could eat with a spoon.
Fred couldn't wash his hair but he could open bottles.

Übung 10.6. **S. 70 / 71**
A: I'm late! Could I use your bike? B: Yes, of course.

A: It's raining. Could I take your umbrella? B: Yes, you can.

A: Mary is at the station. Could I meet her? B: No, you can't.

A: I'm tired. Could I use your pillow? B: Yes, you can.

A: I want to play tennis. Could I use your racket? B: No, you can't.

Übung 10.7. **S. 71**
1. must 2. needn't 3. must – must 4. needn't 5. must – must – must – needn't 6. needn't

Übung 10.8. **S. 72**
Sorry, I can't. I must sweep the floors.
Sorry, I can't. I must do the washing-up.
Sorry, I can't. I must do the cooking.
Sorry, I can't. I must do my homework.
Sorry, I can't. I must go shopping.
Sorry, I can't. I must clean the shoes.

Übung 10.9. S. 72 / 73

1. The car mustn't turn left. It must turn right.
2. The car driver must watch out for the zebra crossing. He must slow down.
3. The cyclist mustn't enter the road. He must drive in the other direction.
4. The car driver mustn't open the door. He must look in the mirror first.
5. The car driver must wait because the other car has the right of way.

Übung 10.10. S. 73

1. There are 10 vehicles: 1 motorbike, 3 cars, 3 lorries, 2 bicycles, 1 bus.
2. We have counted 27 people. And you?
3. There is a supermarket, a café, a shoe shop and a tobacconist.
4. • The driver of the lorry mustn't open the door to the traffic. He must look in the mirror first. (2)
   • The two ladies mustn't stand and talk on the zebra crossing. (3)
   • The driver of the car mustn't park before the zebra crossing. (4)
   • The girl on the bike mustn't hold onto the lorry. (5)
   • Fred mustn't let his dog loose. It mustn't run onto the road. (6)
   • The driver of the sports car mustn't overtake the other car on a crossing. (7)
   • The two children mustn't ride their bikes side by side. (8)

Übung 11.1. S. 75

2. May they sit here?
3. Can I understand everything?
4. Mustn't you smoke here?
5. Will she telephone us later?

Übung 11.2. S. 76

2. The cat is walking on the wall. Is the cat walking on the wall?
3. Mother is cleaning the windows. Is mother cleaning the windows?
4. The children are playing in the playground. Are the children playing in the playground?
5. The lions are running round the cage. Are the lions running round the cage?
6. The boys are getting on the bus. Are the boys getting on the bus?

Übung 11.3. S. 77

1. Is she German?
2. Are you Peter Brown?
3. Is father playing football?
4. Is the window open?
5. May I go out?
6. Must Sheila write a letter?

Übung 11.4. S. 77

2. Does it eat bananas? Yes, it does.
3. Does she fly planes? Yes, she does.
4. Does she go to work? No, she doesn't.
5. Does he sell things? No, he doesn't.

Übung 11.5. S. 77

2. Do you speak English?
3. Does Peter ride his bike?
4. Do I know my headmaster?
5. Do you often go to the cinema?
6. Do teachers mark tests?
7. Does the pilot fly planes?
8. Do we play tennis every summer?
9. Do children like sweets?
10. Does she live on the second floor?

Übung 11.6. S. 78

1C / 2D / 3F / 4L / 5I / 6A / 7B / 8K / 9J / 10E / 11H / 12G

Übung 11.7. S. 79

2. must 3. can't 4. couldn't 5. aren't 6. can't 7. is

Übung 11.8./11.9. S. 80

Individuelle Lösung

Übung 11.10. S. 81
Mr. Brown likes watching TV but he doesn't like going to work.
Mr. Brown likes cleaning his car but he doesn't like doing the washing-up.
Mr. Brown likes listening to music but he doesn't like reading the newspaper.
Mr. Brown likes going out for a walk but he doesn't like driving his car.

Übung 12.1. S. 83
2. What is David doing?
3. What do the bikes need?
4. What are the children playing?

Übung 12.2. S. 83
3. What does Peter buy in the shop?
4. Who do Bob and Pat love?
5. Who does my son meet in town?
6. Who do we like to watch?
7. What do the girls learn?
8. What do they love?
9. Who does father buy a little toy for?
10. What does Mrs. Brown like after lunch?

Übung 12.3. S. 84
Where are you going? I am going to school.
Where are you going? I am going to the sportsground.
Where are you staying? I am staying in church.
Where are you staying? I am staying at home.
Where are you going? I am going to the park.
Where are you staying? I am staying in hospital.
Where are you going? I am going to the pool.

Übung 12.4. S. 84
2. Where does Bob watch television?
3. Where does Mrs. Brown stay every Wednesday?
4. Where do the children go to sing songs?
5. Where do Peter and Pam go for a walk?
6. Where do we swim every weekend?

Übung 12.5. S. 85
2. When do we have tea?
3. When do we help our parents?
4. When does the alarm-clock ring?
5. When do they brush their teeth?

Übung 12.6. S. 85
We get up at a quarter past seven. We have breakfast at half past seven. We go to school at eight. We do our homework at four. We have supper at half past five. We go to bed at twenty-five past nine.

Übung 12.7. S. 86 / 87
1. When 2. Where 3. How 4. How 5. When 6. What 7. What 8. Where 9. When

Übung 12.8. S. 87
Write questions like this:
How often do you go to school by bike?
How often do you watch TV?

Übung 12.9. S. 88
Why – Because – why – Because – why – Because

Übung 12.10. S. 88
Where does she come from?
What is your favourite subject?
How much is all that?
Why can't you come?
When does she get up in the morning?
What is the time now?
Why don't you like him?
Where are you going, Tim?
Where do you go to on Saturdays?
What do you do in your sparetime?
How many eggs does she want?

Übung 12.11. S. 89

2. Who washes the car?
3. Who has a dog?
4. Who likes fish?
5. Who is Brenda's brother?
6. Who can speak English?

Übung 12.12. S. 90

1 / Ann – 2 / Susan – 3 / Bob – 4 / Larry – 5 / Peter – 6 / Jane – 7 / John – 8 / Mother – 9 / Charles – 10 / Mr. Miller – 11 / Bill and Frank are … – 12 / Sarah and Mary are …

Übung 12.13. S. 91

1. Who 2. Where 3. Who 4. Where 5. Where 6. Who 7. Where 8. Who

Übung 12.14. S. 91/92

2. When does the film begin?
3. What does Pat buy?
4. How often have we seen the film?
5. Where does Richard live?
6. Why is Susan very sad?
7. Whose wife is called Mary?
8. How long have they gone to France for?
9. Where are we staying?
10. How much does the bike cost?
11. How does Peter go to school?
12. Who is an assistant in a shop?
13. What does the shop sell?
14. How hard is the last exercise?
15. How many people are at the concert?
16. Why is Thomas happy?
17. Who is playing football?
18. Whose coat is in the bedroom?
19. Who doesn't like spaghetti?
20. How long had we to wait?
21. How much does Fred weigh?
22. What is on the desk?

Übung 12.15. S. 92/93

Individuelle Lösung

Übung 13.1. S. 94

1 train – 2 engine – 3 platform – 4 compartment – 5 station-clock – 6 passengers – 7 newsstand – 8 locker – 9 guard – 10 porter – 11 luggage – 12 suitcase – 13 rails – 14 ticket office

Übung 13.2. S. 95

tickets – trains – on – off – Porters – Passengers – platform – ticket office – tickets – late

Übung 14.1. S. 97

Lösungen Kap. 14

Übung 14.2.
S. 98

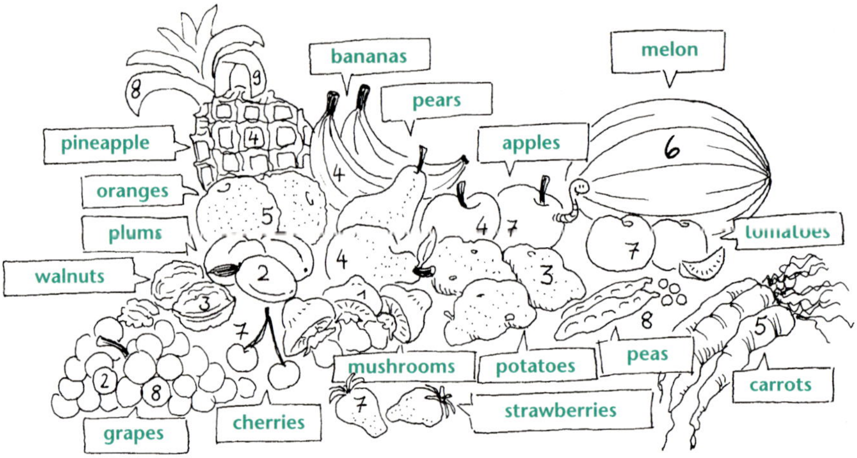

14

Übung 14.3. **S. 98** pineapple – strawberries – tomatoes – bananas – oranges – melon – peas – potatoes – carrots – spinach - pears – grapes – cherries – apples

Übung 14.4. **S. 99** 1. eggs 2. pear 3. milk 4. grapes 5. cucumber 6. pineapple 7. tea 8. butter 9. mushrooms

Übung 14.5. **S. 100**
countables: apple, cornflakes, car, chair, desk, saucer
uncountables: coffee, rice, sugar, orange juice, butter, milk

Übung 14.6. **S. 100** many crackers – much bread – much lemonade – much toast – many tomatoes – many eggs – much sugar – many oranges – much salt – much bacon – much milk – many plates

Übung 14.8. **S. 102 / 103**
True: 2 – 4 – 5 – 7 – 9 – 11
False: 1 – 3 – 6 – 8 – 10

Andy met the old woman on the bus.
She gave Andy three apples.
When Andy got home he had his lunch and did his homework.
He wanted to be strong and tall, famous and rich.
The boys were afraid of Andy and ran away.
Andy didn't know what to say and ran away.
He had a sports car, a helicopter and a big house.
He saw the old woman in his dreams.
He found a small yellow flower.

Übung 14.9. **S. 104**
1. half past seven / breakfast
2. quarter past seven / supper
3. twelve o'clock (noon) / lunch
4. half past four / afternoon tea

Übung 14.10. **S. 104** Individuelle Lösung

Übung 14.11. **S. 105**
Jenny goes sailing every day.
She must get up at half past six.
Mrs. Schröter lays the table for breakfast.

Übung 14.11. S. 105

She puts bread, cheese and meat on the table and sometimes boiled eggs.
The English have ham and eggs, cornflakes with milk, orange juice, toast and marmalade, sausages and tea for breakfast.

Übung 14.12. S. 106

Individuelle Lösung

Übung 14.13. S. 108

W: Can I bring you another slice of bread? Y: Yes, please.

Y: Can I have some more peas, please? W: Of course. Here you are.

W: Would you like another cup of coffee? Y: No, thank you.

W: Some more chicken? Y: No, thank you.

Y: Can I have some more potatoes? And please pass me the pepper.
W: Here you are. But I'm very sorry, the potatoes are off.

Übung 14.14. S. 109 / 110

Individuelle Lösung

Übung 14.15. S. 110 / 111

W: Good afternoon. What can I do for you? Y: Can I have the menu, please.
W: Here it is. Y: Excuse me, waiter, can I order, please.
W: Yes, of course. What would you like to eat? Y: I would like some …
W: Sorry, … are off. Y: Oh, I would like … then.
W: What would you like to drink? Y: …, please.
W: Did you enjoy the meal, sir? Y: Yes, the meal was excellent.
W: Thank you. Would you like some coffee?
Y: No, thank you, but may I have the bill, please?
W: Yes, of course. It's … . Y: Here you are. The tip is for you.
W: Thank you very much. Have a good day. Y: Goodbye.

Übung 15.1. S. 113

Die Sätze folgen alle dem im Beispiel vorgegebenen Muster.

Übung 16.1. S. 114 / 115

bakery – greengrocer's shop – butcher – stationer's shop – chemist's shop – shoeshop – grocer's shop – hairdresser's shop – florist's shop – newsagent's – music store – fishmonger – toy shop – sports shop – jeweller's – supermarket – boutique

Übung 16.2. S. 115

2. Where can you buy meat and sausages? At the butcher's.
3. Where can you buy medicines, pills and toothpaste? At the chemist's.
4. Where can you buy biscuits and cakes? At the baker's.
5. Where can you buy books? At the bookshop.
6. Where can you buy dogs and birds? At the pet shop.
7. Where can you buy tennis rackets and roller skates? At the sportshop.
8. Where can you buy flowers and plants? At the florist's.
9. Where can you buy CDs, CD-players and music instruments? At the music store.
10. Where can you buy watches and rings? At the jeweller's.
11. Where can you buy shirts, coats and dresses? At the boutique.
12. Where can you buy soap, toothpaste, cornflakes and chocolate? At the supermarket.
13. Where can you buy dolls, toy cars and teddy bears? At the toy shop.
14. Where can you buy magazines and newspapers? At the newsagent's.
15. Where can you buy pens, stamps and pencils? At the stationer's.

Lösungen Kap. 16 +18

16 + 18

Übung 16.3. S. 116 Individuelle Lösung nach dem Vorbild des Beispiels.

Übung 16.4. S. 118 1C: a tube of toothpaste – 2A: a packet of cigarettes – 3E: a box of cigars – 4G: a jar of jam – 5K: a bottle of milk – 6N: a bar of chocolate – 7B: a piece of chalk – 8D: a pound of sugar – 9M: a cup of tea – 10F: a pair of shoes – 11L: a tin of beans – 12J: a glass of wine – 13I: a sack of potatoes – 14H: a loaf of bread

Übung 16.5. S. 118 two jars of jam – a dozen eggs – four slices of cake – a bottle of lemonade – a pound of cherries – a slice of cheese – a loaf of bread – a carton of milk – a chicken – three tins of fish – two packets of tea – a bar of chocolate

Übung 16.6. S. 119 supermarket – shopping list – hand – trolley – one pound of apples – three bars of chocolate – three bananas – a bottle of milk – six eggs – tea bags – basket – party – ice-cream – hand – duck – mouse – shelf – pencil-case – three pencils – one fountain pen – three ballpoint pens – writing-pad – pencil-case – box of sweets – chocolate – pencil-case – shoulder – pocket

Übung 16.7. S. 121
Y: I'd like three bottles of milk, please.
Y: Yes, half a pound of tomatoes, please.
Y: No, I need three tins of beans, too.
Y: All right, how much is that altogether?
Y: Thank you. Goodbye.

Übung 16.8. S. 122
Y: A pound of butter, one bottle of milk and ten eggs for the lady, please.
Y: Do you sell meat and sausages?
Y: Half a pound of ham, please – and where can we buy meat?
Y: Thank you. Can we have a packet of tea, half a pound of coffee and a bottle of orange juice, please?
Y: Have you got any sweets?
Y: Two bars of chocolate, please.
Y: That's all, thank you. How much is it?

Übung 16.9. S. 123
Children's wear: Du hast sicher gemerkt: In diesem Kaufhaus gibt es keine Kinderkleidung.
Sportswear: ball – boxing gloves
Radio / Television: record player – records – radio – TV-set
Toys: doll – ball – teddy bear
Shoes: slippers – boots – shoes
Ladies' wear: dress – pullover – coat – hat
Men's wear: pyjamas – hat – suit – tie
Books: books – magazines – comics
Stationery: writing-pad – ruler – rubber – pencils
Pets: budgie – dog – cat – rabbit – parrot
Food: butter – cheese – milk – bread
Tools: scissors – hammer

Übung 18.1. S. 127 2. it flies 3. she gets 4. he fetches 5. it does 6. she buys 7. it catches 8. he cooks 9. she hurries 10. he goes 11. she kisses

Übung 18.2.
S. 127

Fred sometimes listens to CDs with friends. He often reads books. Fred seldom plays football in the school team and he never does housework. He usually watches TV in the evening.
Susan never listens to CDs on Mondays. She never plays football but sometimes she reads books. She seldom helps with the housework and sometimes she watches pop shows on TV.
Peter listens to CDs every day. He seldom reads books and never plays football. He is a good boy. Every day he does housework and he often likes watching action movies on TV.

Übung 18.3.
S. 128

Write sentences like these:
He seldom washes the dishes. He cleans the floor every week. He does the shopping and washes the car every week, too. Every day he sets the table, he makes breakfast and the beds and he tidies the bedroom. Every month he waters the flowers and cleans the shoes. He never empties the dustbin and washes his clothes.

Übung 18.4.
S. 128 / 129

The earth goes round the sun once a year. The moon goes round the earth once a month. The earth spins on its axis once a day.

Übung 18.5.
S. 129

His name is David. He is thirty years old. He comes from Great Britain and lives in London. He lives in a flat which has six rooms. He works in a big school as a teacher. He speaks English and German. He is married and has four children. He likes football and fishing and he hates Italy, boxing, watching TV, beer and warm milk. In his spare time he plays tennis and he collects stamps and old records.

Übung 18.6.
S. 130

housewife – teacher – bus driver – fireman – farmer – car mechanic – psychiatrist – actor – manager – butcher – cook – nurse – gardener – secretary – dentist – chimney sweep – electrician – veterinarian – artist – doctor – painter – shop assistant – waitress – technician – plumber – dock worker – carpenter – builder – engineer – clerk

Übung 18.7.
S. 131

A teacher is a person who teaches. A sailor is a person who works on a ship. A housewife or houseman is a person who does the housework. A farmer is a person who works in the fields. A worker is a person who works in a factory. A taxi-driver is a person who takes people from one place to another. A painter is a person who paints houses and doors. A secretary is a person who types letters. A waiter or a waitress is a person who brings you tee food in a restaurant. A car mechanic is a person who repairs cars. A test pilot is a person who flies new planes. A doctor is a person who finds out what's the matter with you when you're ill. A chimney sweep is a person who cleans the chimney. A football player is a person who must be very good at playing football. A policeman is a person who stops cars which go too fast. A bus driver is a person who drives a bus. A cleaner is a person who cleans other people's houses. A dentist is a person who helps you when you've got a toothache. A cook is a person who makes meals. A shop assistant is a person who sells things in a shop. A nurse is a person who helps the doctor. A dock worker is a person who repairs ships. A postman is a person who brings the letters. A carpenter is a person who makes furniture. A baker is a person who makes bread and cakes.

Übung 18.9. **S. 133**

Fred stretches his arms. He rubs his eyes and gets out of bed. Then Fred goes to the bathroom. After that he washes his hands and his face. Finally he has a shower. Then he dries his body with a towel. Afterwards he puts on his shirt and his trousers. Then he goes downstairs to the kitchen. There he sits down at the breakfast table and has breakfast. At last Fred leaves the house and goes to the bus stop.

Übung 18.10. **S. 134**

The dog wags its tail. Then the bell rings. The hen lays an egg. The egg falls into a net. After that the revolver fires. It makes a hole in the fishtank. Then the water pours down. Finally the sleeping boy wakes up.

Übung 18.11. **S. 134**

Individuelle Lösung

Übung 19.1. **S. 137**

I played football. I visited the zoo. I looked out of the window. I visited Mr. Brown. I washed our car. I watched TV. I phoned Mary. I played tennis. I walked in the park. I helped an old lady to cross the road. I jumped into the pool. I repaired my radio. I carried the bags home from the shop. I prepared breakfast.

Übung 19.2. **S. 137**

robbed – watched – phoned – stopped – tried – dropped – grabbed – arrested

Übung 19.3. **S. 138**

wash	washed
play	played
visit	visited
look	looked
watch	watched
phone	phoned
walk	walked
carry	carried
prepare	prepared

jump	jumped
help	helped
repair	repaired
rob	robbed
stop	stopped
try	tried
drop	dropped
grab	grabbed
arrest	arrested

Übung 19.4. **S. 138 / 139**

3 – 9 – 1 – 15 – 10 – 8 – 13 – 14 – 6 – 7 – 2 – 5 – 4 – 11 – 12

Fred woke up. He heard a noise. He switched on the light, then he got out of his bed. He put on his dressing gown and opened the bedroom door. He went downstairs. Then he listened at the door. He opened the door and suddenly saw a cat outside the window. Then he went upstairs again and took off his dressing gown. He got into bed, switched off the light and went to sleep again.

Übung 19.5. **S. 139 / 140**

was – moon – were – house – said – answered – said – opened – door – walked – followed – was – dark – couldn't – was – scream – shouted – felt – hand – neck – turned – saw – ghost – was – was – candle – shouted – appeared – blood – skeleton – asked – said – was

Übung 19.6.
S. 141

1 bit	3 brought	7 led	10 drank
11 ran	12 chose	13 threw	15 said
16 dug	17 drew	18 held	23 understood
25 sold	26 met	29 shot	29 thought
31 felt	34 kept	35 slept	36 sat

1 broke	2 lit	3 began	4 gave
5 forgot	6 sang	7 left	8 grew
9 told	12 caught	14 rode	15 shrank
18 hid	19 lay	20 lost	21 fought
22 went	24 shook	27 bought	28 spoke
30 taught	31 fell	32 laid	

19

Übung 19.7.
S. 143

Form sentences like these:
A: What was your weekend like?
B: It was very exciting.
A: What did you do on Saturday?
B: Last Saturday I made breakfast for my whole family. Then I went on an outing with friends. We had lunch at a nice little pond and went swimming.
A: Did you do the washing-up, too?
B: Yes, I did the washing-up after breakfast.

Übung 19.8.
S. 144

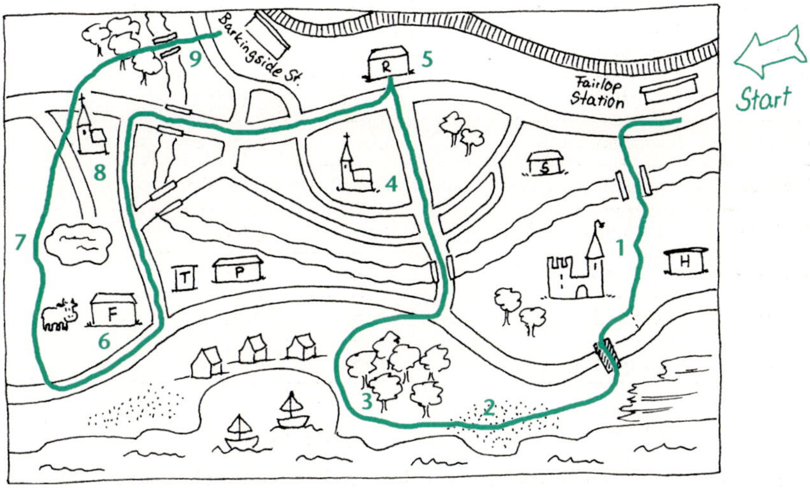

Übung 19.9.
S. 145

Form sentences like these:
A: Fred, how was your holiday?
F: It was quite good.
A: What was the weather like?
F: The weather was fantastic. It was warm and sunny all day long.
A: And how was the bed in your hotel?
F: Oh, well, it was a little bit too short.
…

Übung 19.10., 19.11.
S. 146 / 147

Individuelle Lösung

Lösungen Kap. 19–20

19
+
20

Übung 19.12.
S. 148–150

1 lived – 2 had – 3 was – 4 had – 5 was – 6 spent – 7 was – 8 was – 9 went – 10 used – 11 threw – 12 fell – 13 began – 14 thought – 15 cried – 16 wept – 17 heard – 18 looked – 19 was – 20 coudn't – 21 was – 22 said – 23 said – 24 answered – 25 said – 26 went – 27 thought – 28 was – 29 wanted – 30 said – 31 dived – 32 came – 33 threw – 34 was – 35 picked – 36 laughed – 37 threw – 38 caught – 39 turned – 40 ran – 41 called – 42 hopped – 43 didn't – 44 kept – 45 was – 46 ate – 47 came – 48 jumped – 49 got – 50 knocked – 51 cried – 52 ran – 53 was – 54 saw – 55 was – 56 was – 57 closed – 58 went – 59 saw – 60 was – 61 asked – 62 answered – 63 asked – 64 told – 65 promised – 66 could – 67 said – 68 thought – 69 was – 70 cried – 71 lost – 72 played – 73 dived – 74 found – 75 returned – 76 said – 77 went – 78 opened – 79 returned – 80 hopped – 81 sat – 82 said – 83 didn't – 84 told – 85 was – 86 said – 87 did – 88 touched – 89 enjoyed – 90 ate – 91 turned – 92 said – 93 burst – 94 didn't – 95 couldn't – 96 grew – 97 spoke – 98 said – 99 had – 100 put – 101 got – 102 turned – 103 spoke – 104 said – 105 began – 106 went – 107 knew – 108 had – 109 picked – 110 climbed – 111 put – 112 turned – 113 had – 114 smiled – 115 told – 116 told – 117 asked – 118 looked – 119 went – 120 were – 121 lived

Übung 20.1.
S. 152

Susie has forgotten a telephone number. Harriet has broken a window. Trish and Johnny have played tennis. Mrs. Smith has missed the bus. Bob has had an accident. Tom has cut his finger. Harriet has lost her key. Mrs. Smith has washed her car. Sunny has got a letter. Mac has found money.

Übung 20.2.
S. 153

take	took	taken
forget	forgot	forgotten
come	came	come
feed	fed	fed
speak	spoke	spoken
see	saw	seen
give	gave	given
pay	paid	paid
write	wrote	written
do	did	done
go	went	gone
break	broke	broken

Übung 20.3.
S. 154

I have had breakfast (12) – I've brushed my teeth (2) – I have washed myself (9) – I've gone to school (8) – I've had lunch (5) – I have cleaned my bike (4) – I've taken the dog for a walk (11) – I have taken photos (10) – I've drunk lemonade (3) – I've ridden my bike (14) – I have played with my friend (1) – I have relaxed (6) – I've played football (15) – I've had dinner (13) – I have watched TV (7)

Übung 20.4. S. 155

Have you ever:
seen a ghost – seen yourself on TV – ridden a camel – kissed your teacher – been to Great Britain – smoked – forgotten your homework – lost your key – slept in a tent – been to Africa – lost money – had a rabbit – been wounded – planted a tree

Übung 20.5. S. 156 / 157

He is doing the washing-up. – He has done the washing-up.
He is drying the dishes. – He has dried the dishes.
He is watering the flowers. – He has watered the flowers.
He is making the beds. – He has made the beds.
He is washing the clothes. – He has washed the clothes.
He is cleaning the windows. – He has cleaned the windows.
He is cooking dinner. – He has cooked dinner.
He is laying the table. – He has laid the table.

Übung 20.6. S. 157

P: I haven't cleaned my shoes yet. – I haven't brushed my teeth yet. – I haven't found my warm sweater yet. – I haven't phoned Anne yet and told her that we are late. – I haven't packed my suitcase yet.

Übung 20.7. S. 158

since	**for**
last week	two hours
1990	two years
Monday	a few seconds
1st May	five minutes
Easter	a long time
our first meeting	
one o'clock	

Übung 20.8. S. 159

1. have lived / have been living 2. has been 3. has lived / has been living 4. haven't seen 5. have had 6. has been 7. has had 8. have been learning

Übung 20.9. S. 159

2. for 3. for 4. since 5. for 6. for 7. for 8. for – since

Übung 20.10. S. 160

1. has written 2. haven't cleaned 3. have cleaned – has done 4. have – shown 5. Have – eaten 6. have seen 7. have never seen 8. have always wanted 9. have – done 10. has flown 11. has arrived 12. have had 13. Have – ever seen 14. have already bought 15. hasn't written 16. hasn't lost 17. have already had 18. haven't finished

Übung 21.1. S. 162

Stephanie is going to take her dog for a walk. Paul and Frank are going to help in the garden. We are going to meet our school friends. Sandra and Elisabeth are going to watch a western film. Jenny is going to wash our car. I'm going to ride my bike. Dad and I are going to play football.

Übung 21.2. S. 162

Individuelle Lösung

Lösungen Kap. 21–22

Übung 21.3.
S. 163

York, 30-11-1998
Dear Pat,
It's my birthday next Saturday and I'm going to have a party. Can you come? I hope so! We'll have food and games, lots of fun and lots of prizes. The party starts at four o'clock. See you on Saturday!
Lots of love
Joanne

Übung 21.4.
S. 163

Wir haben zuerst alle Beiträge nummeriert. Die Reihenfolge lautet dann:
6 / 18 / 3 / 16 / 13 / 9 / 1 / 7 / 4 / 11 / 14 / 17 / 5 / 2 / 8 / 10 / 15 / 12

Übung 21.5.
S. 164 / 165

Mark will take some cassettes. Ruth will go to the hairdresser's first. Jack will buy a new dress. Brad will go with a friend. Tom and Jerry will dance with the girls. Brenda will take some chocolate. Margaret will put on her best clothes. Peter will take a bottle of cola. Linda and Sue will play games. Malcolm will go home after 12 o'clock.

Übung 21.6., 21.7., 21.8.
S. 165 / 166

Individuelle Lösungen

Kapitel 22
S. 167 / 168

Individuelle Lösungen